LOSING SELF, FINDING GOD, FINDING LIFE

# KILLING THE CEO

DARREN COPLAND

Ark House Press
arkhousepress.com

© 2025 Darren Copland

Unless otherwise stated, all Scriptures are taken from the NIV Study Bible (10th Anniversary Edition ed.). Barker k, B. D. (1995). Grand Rapids: Zondervan Publishing House.

*Some names and identifying details have been changed to protect the privacy of individuals.*

Cataloguing in Publication Data:
Title: Killing the CEO
ISBN: 978-1-7638801-0-8 (pbk)
Subjects: REL108030    RELIGION / Christian Living / Leadership & Mentoring; REL012170    RELIGION / Christian Living / Personal Memoirs; PSY036000 PSYCHOLOGY / Mental Health;

Design by initiateagency.com

*"For whoever would save his life will lose it, but whoever loses his life for my sake will find it. For what will it profit a man if he gains the whole world and forfeits his soul?"*
Matthew 16:25 – 26

*For Jesus, Yvette and my family*

# CHARACTER REFERENCES

My first close connection to Darren was when he sought me out as a sounding board during his transition to large organisational responsibilities and leadership. This was over 10 years ago. His humility and integrity as a leader impressed me at this point and has continued to do so as he's facilitated expansion and organisational change, which can generate some of the tougher challenges of Christian leadership.

I saw him walk through the 'valley of the shadow' with executive stress and he has emerged stronger and more defined than ever, with a message that will help all those courageous enough to take on big organisational mandates and determine to take them to their fruition.

In the middle of all this he has raised a wonderful family together with his equally amazing wife, Yvette. He is straightforward and pragmatic in his approach to both people and problems, a visionary with a heart for people's healthy, sustainable development.

**Chris Mulhare**
**Senior Pastor, New Hope Church Toowoomba**

I have had the privilege of knowing Darren and his wife Yvette for the past six years. Over this time, we have developed a strong friendship and shared many meaningful conversations about life, faith, and problem-solving. Together, we co-facilitate regular events for leaders and business professionals in our local church, aiming to help them integrate Kingdom principles into the workplace.

In recent years, Darren has become a mentor to me, providing invaluable guidance on the practical aspects of building small businesses and managing teams. His insights have challenged me to reflect on my own blind spots and foster a healthy organisational culture within the entities I lead.

I had the honour of walking alongside Darren during his transformative journey of "losing self, finding God, and finding life", which ultimately inspired the creation of this book. Darren is an exceptional communicator and facilitator, bringing authenticity and depth to his training. His leadership is marked by a humility that has been refined over time, making his approach both refreshing and genuine.

This book offers a step-by-step guide through his journey, candidly exploring the highs and lows while providing practical solutions to the challenges you may be facing.

**Dr Jeremy Fernando MBChB, BMedSc,**
**FANZCA, FCICM, GChPOM**
**Anaesthetist, Intensivist and Perioperative Medical Specialist**
**Director of Intensive Care and Clinical Lead of the Perioperative**
**Care Service at St Vincent's Private Hospital, Toowoomba**
**Co-Director of MyProcedure – A Perioperative Care Company**

Darren Copland is the real deal. Having known him since he was a teenager as a family friend, I have witnessed him grow through many challenges that would have tested the best of us; including the years he spent educating teens in the classroom, including my own, and his lengthy stint as the CEO he eventually set out to kill! He is a family man who has always remained faithful to his convictions, especially the ones he has expressed in this book. There has never been a time when I have questioned his integrity, nor his ability to inspire others to catch something of the bigger divine picture. For those aspiring to be, in the words of Christ, 'made whole', this book can position you to set off in the right direction.

**Geoffrey Gay**
**Retired educator and author of *LostRalia***

I have known Darren for over eight years through his role as CEO of one of Christian Venues Association's (CVA) leading venues. Darren also served CVA with genuine authenticity, intelligence and honesty in his role as Company Secretary. His relational leadership style enabled him to identify and discuss the core issues of governance and effective leadership and our association is better for his contribution. Darren has also presented workshops at our national conferences and is a gifted communicator.
Walking alongside Darren through some of his journey, I am excited to see this book released and know that it will reflect Darren's genuine desire to help others.

**Graeme Janes**
**Chief Executive Officer, 2016 - present**
**Christian Venues Association**

Leading significant change in any organisation is not easy, but it is what Darren applied his high-level passion, genuine authenticity and significant energy to achieve, but in the end, it was at the high cost of his own health. What he discovered though this major life trauma cannot be found in a "Seminar" or in a "How to" book, but rather he has laid bare his journey for us to absorb and learn from. If you are a leader of people, the issue of Mental Health will be "front and center" for you at some point, and therefore this is a priceless book. Don't put it down!

I have known Darren for over 30 years as his chairperson, a fellow director, and most importantly, as a trusted friend. I have had a front-row seat to this remarkable journey, and I can attest to his honesty, integrity and his strong personal faith, which has seen him humbly walking through to a new examined life.

**Greg Anderson**
**Chair, Highway Church, Ormeau, Qld**
**Director, Delport & Anderson Pty Ltd**

I have known Darren for over 15 years, having first connected through our mutual involvement with high schools. Over the years, our friendship has grown, and I deeply appreciate Darren's honesty, care for others, wisdom, and leadership experience. The way he has navigated the past few years is a genuine reflection of his character—he leads by example and consistently lives out his beliefs. I wholeheartedly recommend him to you.

**Peter Sondergeld**
**Lead Pastor - Restoration Church Toowoomba**
**Author of Becoming You: Becoming the**
**Person God Made You to Be**

Darren is a long-standing friend and trusted colleague of over 20 years. We have worked as educational colleagues in independent schools, and each lead our own educational organisations. Together, we have embraced the roles of organisational leadership, including vision casting, professional development, corporate governance, fundraising and event management. Our common values have been authentic leadership, entrepreneurial endeavours, and maximizing human development. Darren's focus has been around the adventure education model, while mine has been a senior school, which has benefited from its unique approach to character development in young people. Under his leadership, the organisation he led more than doubled its capacity, with approximately 20,000 young people taking part in tailored programs by 2022.

Darren has dedicated his life to enhancing the capacity of others' lives and helping them become their best possible selves. He leads by example with integrity, courage, innovation and a servant heart. Darren lives these values with passion and authenticity, and it is his disposition to service that empowers others to plan their lives for high-impact outcomes.

Leaders should be both readers and communicators. Darren is both. He would be one of the most poignant and impactful public communicators I have experienced. I have engaged his communication skills many times at formal dinners, professional development programs and young people's events. His reading of local context and understanding of market dynamics have provided high impact material for his storytelling.

**Mark Hands**
**Retired CEO – The Industry School (2006 – 2024)**

# CONTENTS

# PREFACE

Stories are powerful. They allow us to connect personally with the characters, events, and emotions evoked by the situations that occur. A well-crafted tale has us hanging on every word, always hopeful of a preferred outcome.

Jesus was perhaps the greatest storyteller of all time, providing an unparalleled depth of insight through his perceptive selection and delivery of parables[1]. The Jewish tradition of listening deeply to this oral teaching enhanced the transformative power of these parables. The practice of listening deeply is about discovering identity and answering the embedded question of who am I in this story? Take some time and read the parable of the prodigal son and ask yourself the question: who do I identify with most? Are you the prodigal? Are you the brother, the father, the mother? Are you the owner of the pig pen?

Hollywood has mastered the art of crafting powerful stories with heroes, villains, intriguing plots, and a climactic experience of some sort and when we watch a movie, we typically picture ourselves as the main character, facing our own internal struggles, saving the day, and becoming the hero. However, the more perceptive among us might realise that we are not always the centre of the story. Our connections are often false and aspira-

---

[1]  *A parable is a simple story used to illustrate a deeper truth, true to life not history.*

tional at best. We might not always be the best or nicest person and sadly we are rarely the hero. Perhaps more often than not, we are the villain - we just don't want to admit it. The truth remains that there is transformative power when we listen deeply, face reality and correctly identify who we are in the story. If we are not who we would like to be, then we need the courage to face reality and embark on our own journey of transformation.

*Killing the CEO* is my story, written from my perspective. It details my journey from being a competent and successful CEO of an outdoor education company to a state of complete physical, mental, and spiritual burnout. On the journey, I faced incredibly high levels of stress and anxiety and was diagnosed with a major depressive disorder. After two and half years of fighting against what was going on beneath the surface, with deep soul searching and reflection, and after venting at and arguing with God, I surrendered completely. And it was not until this point of surrender that I truly realised that I had been living a false identity. I fully believed that I was the CEO, and trying to live up to the expectations of this false identity almost killed me. By surrendering completely to God, I began to discover my true identity and follow his path of transformation.

I hope my story can be a parable for you. I implore you to listen deeply, to see where you might be just like me, to feel the emotional pain and sense the depth of heartache caused by stress, depression and anxiety that results from trying to be someone or something you are not, and from trying to live up to the expectations of a false identity. And most of all, I would love you to embrace the hope and transformation that can only be realised when we find our true identity in Christ.

## DISCLAIMERS:

I love the company I worked for and led as the CEO. It is one of the best outdoor education centres in the country. Its mode of delivery and the outcomes achieved are extraordinary. I 100% believe in its mission, purpose, and people.

As you would know, any time you have a group of people together, you will all face challenges and all make mistakes: interpersonal, intrapersonal, departmental, vertical, horizontal, from within and without. The company I led was no exception. During my tenure some individuals departed, some were dismissed, and some remained, but every person involved was the perfect person for that season and added their own flavour to the next chapter.

I have no desire to point fingers of blame or to paint anyone in a negative light. The stories I share are extremely painful and often still raw and are included to highlight the key moments and events in my journey, how I processed them and what it has taken to find the way forward. These stories have involved the very people who were serving the vision of the company alongside me and following my leadership and I have used pseudonyms to protect the identity of those involved. The Chair of the Board, the Directors and the Executive deserve credit for my successful transition out of the company whilst maintaining strong relationships. For that, I am extremely grateful.

## ENGAGE WITH THE PROCESS:

Throughout this journey, a major processing tool for me was journalling. I would spend some time most days reflecting on how I felt, the intensity of the fight, what I was thinking about and if I had any moments of revelation. Journalling provided me with the opportunity to throw up a range of questions and challenge my thinking. Sometimes, I just vented, and at other times, I just recorded the actions of a given day. Often, the entry would turn into a prayer. I have included many direct excerpts from my own journal to authentically illustrate my raw and battered mental state.

Although the journal entries and excerpts have been presented chronologically, I'm sure you can understand that I did not necessarily process things in a sequential manner. My processing was complex, complicated, and messy as I was struggling, fighting, and questioning everything all at once. What this means for you is that some of the entries reflect the content in the previous chapters whilst others are covered in later chapters. I'm more than confident that you can handle it.

At the end of each chapter there is an opportunity for you to pause and reflect, to answer some questions and to be honest with yourself and where you are right now. Use this book as a resource and inspiration to begin your own journey of reflection that leads to transformation. Journalling is a powerful tool. Please resist the urge to just read through without taking stock of your own situation.

Also, please don't make the mistake of thinking that this book, my journalling, or your journalling is only useful in tough times. If you are reading this book and life is going well, then praise God. However, I challenge you to consider what you might be grateful for. Who could you be looking out for? How could you contribute to the well-being of those around you? We are all on a journey of transformation, and there is a time for everything under the sun. Engage with the process of journalling, spend time in reflection and experience the transformative power of this process.

My wholehearted intent for penning this journey is to connect with you and perhaps help you on your own journey. After all, a wise person learns from others' mistakes. You may not be the CEO of a company, and you may not even be in a position of leadership. However, I would venture to guess that you, a little like me, believe that you are the CEO of your own life. You know what you want. You know what you think, and you're prepared to move towards the things that light you up inside. As you will discover, the false identity of the CEO had gained complete control of my entire life. Essentially, I did not exist outside of my role and my work, and it was only through a lot of pain that I realised I had to change. If I did not kill the CEO, I would cease to exist and never become the person I was created to be. For me this story is not fictional. It is quite literally life and death.

If you can relate to my story or even parts of it, then I sincerely hope that the journey, revelations, insights, and strategies I share may shine some light on the path you're treading. And in this light, I hope it encourages you to take the actions necessary to find God, and in him to find your true self and then align your path with your goals, passion, purpose, and calling.

# INTRODUCTION

# "I AM THE CEO!"

It was 1.30 pm on Wednesday the 25th of August 2021, and I was in a bad way, both mentally and physically. I had a deep, heavy, and intense burning pain in my chest, and I was totally exhausted. My eyes were dark and sunken. It looked like I had gone a few rounds in the boxing ring and felt like an utter failure, I was at a loss for what to do next. I just knew I needed help and after all, this meeting was my idea. I had asked my doctor for a referral to see a psychologist.

It was awkward. I was awkward. I didn't know where to sit. I didn't know how to sit. Should I relax and lean back or sit upright? Do I sit with my legs crossed or uncrossed? Which tells a better story? Do I sit in the single seat? Or do I sit on the couch? Sitting in the wrong place may give off an impression of overconfidence or even arrogance. If I lean back on the couch, I'll come across as relaxed and he'll wonder if I really need help. If I lie down on the couch, he'll probably assume that I am a total basket case. There were no rules or even suggestions about where to sit, but I kind of knew what was going to happen. I sat on the couch. My body language betrayed any sense of control or composure I thought I had. I was terrified. I clenched my jaw and fists and crossed my arms and legs. I sat uneasily on the corner of the couch, as far away from the psychologist as possible.

If it were possible to sit on the other side of the couch, closer to the wall, I probably would have sat there.

It was at this point that my psychologist, Virgil, asked me to tell him about myself. The words, **"I am the CEO"** flew out of my mouth without hesitation or forethought. I was being as honest as possible and for me, there seemed no other explanation necessary. Being the CEO was not just my role at work, it was who I was. I was the CEO!

## THERE WAS NO DISTINCTION BETWEEN MY ROLE AND MY IDENTITY

It was obvious from day one that Virgil could see more of the picture than I realised. The fear of being psychoanalysed was no longer just a fear, or something that happened in the movies. It was happening to me in real time on the edge of his couch, and yes, much to my embarrassment, despite intending only to talk about my job and my role, I did find myself sitting on a couch and talking about my childhood, my parents, and particularly my Dad.

To my complete surprise, right from my first session, Virgil was not buying everything I was selling. He didn't mock me, or belittle me, but his fine-tuned listening skills picked up on one of the core issues in my first four words… "I am the CEO." He was determined to discover the root of this statement, this belief. At first, his line of questioning didn't make sense to me. The discussion went something like:

**Virgil:** "What do you mean when you say I am the CEO?"

**Darren:** "That is me, that is who I am, it is what I do" (after all we are what we do right? Why else is that everyone's question when you meet them for the first time?)

**Virgil:** "So you are telling me that before you were the CEO, there was no Darren?"

| | |
|---|---|
| **Darren:** | "Well no… of course not, but… " |
| **Virgil**: | "That would be insane! Wouldn't it? …" |

Wow, the first session, spilling my heart out on a psychologist's couch, practicing unparalleled vulnerability and the one person who is supposed to help me suggests I might be in danger of being certified insane. That's a bit rough!

I saw Virgil regularly, at least once a month and sometimes more over the next two and a half years. As you may have guessed, things got a lot worse before there were any signs of getting better.

The problem was that I believed I was telling the truth. "**I AM** the CEO."

I felt called by God to serve the company. I loved the vision, the mission, and was so passionate about everything we stood for. I was one with the role, and it was one with me. Do you understand the privilege of working in a place where everything lines up? Your goals, your vision, your personal mission, your values, your beliefs, your way of doing things? I was living the dream! I never had to go to work. I was just doing what I loved, for a cause I believed in, and I was getting paid to do it. Not only that, but I was also now in the position of driving the company forward into all it could be. It was dawning on me that my entire identity, purpose, current reality, and foreseeable future were all inextricably entwined with my role as CEO.

In all honesty, from my perspective, Darren did not exist outside of the role of being the CEO.

I had been fighting a losing battle for a long time, and I was exhausted. For the first time in my life, I felt like I had been 'knocked down'. I literally felt like a concussed boxer, as if someone had just hit me flush on the jaw, and I was stumbling on the canvas, trying to steady myself to let the referee know I was ready for another round. Inspired by Rocky Balboa's famous quote, I was determined to win... *"It is not how hard you can hit. It is how hard you can get hit and keep moving forward. That's how winning is done."* For me, this was not just a brilliant line in a movie - this was truth, this was reality.

With gentle prompting from Virgil, I added some more layers of paint to the canvas of my life. I explained a little about the organisation I worked for and how long I had been there, and I told him how much I loved to work and serve a mission greater than myself. I mentioned I was a driven person, but that others might describe me as an overachieving, task-driven perfectionist. I told Virgil that if I put my mind to something, especially if I'd been given any kind of responsibility, almost nothing could prevent me from achieving it. I also mentioned the exceedingly high expectations and standards I had for myself, and the organisation I was leading. I had my dream job, where I worked every day with passion and commitment.

Work was easy. It was a gift. As the old saying goes, you don't have to go to work when you love what you do, and that's how I ended up as CEO. I'd worked my way up in an organisation I loved and believed in with a team I cared about and considered family. I shared how my professional career had transitioned from teaching Physical Education in the late '90s and into the early 2000s when I became an outdoor educator. In this role I facilitated team building and leadership programs for tens of thousands of young people and staff along the way. With increasing skills and management experience, I earned promotions within the company and eventually reached the position of CEO in 2013. In my 10 years in this role, the company effectively doubled in size, turnover and impact. By restructuring the company, enhancing our governance, and being fully committed to our strategic plan, we created a fantastic culture and successfully navigated the perils of doing business during the COVID-19 pandemic. We were actively looking to expand, and there was a sense of excitement and anticipation in the air.

But as the CEO, I was cooked!

Darren, the 47-year-old husband of Yvette, my wife of 26 years, and the father of four fantastic children, Sam, Jack, Harry, and Bella was cooked too. But talking about that was much deeper and took more prompting, not because I didn't have any feelings or see the problems there, but because I wanted to fix the work problem first. Afterall, I was the CEO! Virgil dug deeper and asked about my family of origin, my extended family, and so on. I briefly covered off on some of my interests and hobbies, such as playing and coaching AFL and more recently, paddle boarding and mountain biking. Virgil appeared genuinely interested in me and he continued to inquire gently about my current mental, physical, social, and spiritual health. He wanted to know everything.

Virgil didn't want to talk to the CEO. He wanted to talk to Darren. Why was Darren sitting awkwardly on his couch seeking his help?

**Apparently, I am more than the CEO.**

## FIGHTING THE UNKNOWN

The problem was this battle for my identity had been raging for years and I had not even realised I was in a fight. I didn't even know who or what I was fighting against. I just knew that If I didn't start winning soon, I might not get up off the canvas. The focus of this battle shifted away from inspirational leadership, vision, goals, and success and became a battle for my very survival. This was a battle for my soul, my identity.

Unfortunately, this fundamental belief that 'I am the CEO' was entirely untrue. It was a false identity, a false self that had become so entangled with the core of who I believed I was that I could not see any other alternative. I couldn't see the truth. Every thought, action, and behaviour reinforced the belief that I was the CEO. The CEO had taken over every facet of my life without challenge and fully believed he was in control. And truth be told, the CEO was killing me! The battle was real and the consequences potentially catastrophic.

## LONG STORY SHORT – IF THE CEO WINS, I DIE.

I'm not trying to be melodramatic here. But left unchecked, the result of the CEO running my life and trying to meet his expectations could well have led to my end. The depths of depression, peaks of anxiety and the burn of stress can all end in physical death. These, when combined with the dangerous habits of self-medication, poor diet, lack of exercise and sleep deprivation, can end in physical death. Let's just say the battle was real.

If I did not die physically, and the CEO won the battle for my identity, I would be stuck forever living a false reality. Working harder and longer with less satisfaction. The CEO's appetite for success would enslave me, driving me to perfection and focusing on whatever was next. Satisfaction for a job well done or a task complete was not part of the CEO's psyche. I would become a shell of my former self, a shadow of who I was meant to be, all the while believing I was serving God and being the best I could be.

## IF DARREN WINS, I LIVE – I GET MY LIFE BACK.

If I win, I discover, or perhaps rediscover, who Darren is. And I get the joy of becoming the best version of myself in every facet of my life. I'm free to just be me and do whatever I choose. If I win, the CEO becomes a lived experience with lessons and wisdom that can help release me into a much healthier future.

If I win, I might just find God and my true self. I might begin to live a life of abundance reflecting my true identity as someone who is loved by

God and chosen to partner with him in bringing the Kingdom of Heaven to reality here on earth.

As I recall some of the key moments, incidents, interactions, beliefs, and revelations of my story, I simply ask you to consider your own lens of perception. What sunglasses might you be wearing? I suspect that although we all have frames that suit us perfectly, some of us might wear similar lenses. For example, if you like to work hard and achieve, and you are driven to succeed and like to do things perfectly, or at the very least exceptionally well - if you love to serve, lead, and connect with like-minded people, to share vision, to inspire others, to live with purpose and for a purpose, and If you believe you are on the planet for a reason and will do all you can to fulfill your calling. Or if you struggle to rest and have a constant desire to be productive and useful, and you want to be part of something bigger than yourself, then chances are, we might be looking at life through similar lenses. You and I might have more in common than you would care to admit. And perhaps some of my experiences, insights and revelations will help you as you navigate your own journey.

As you journey with me, I hope you see that killing the CEO was my only option. It may also be yours.

# P A R T 1

······································································································

## THE RISE OF THE CEO

# CHAPTER 1

# MEET DARREN AND THE CEO

## HARD WORK AND GETTING TO THE OTHER SIDE OF THE TRACKS

I love my family. We are close and have always had strong positive relationships across the board. I grew up in a loving home, with Mum, Dad and two brothers. I was the middle child and for the most part, life was good. Our parents were strong faithful Christians and my brothers and I would make early decisions in life to follow Christ. As time passed, our faith became our own and we each progressed and matured. We would go to church most Sundays and understood the importance of positive connections with a community of believers. Bible studies and prayer meetings were the norm, and we knew how to host a gathering. We mostly lived in rental properties, ranging from farmhouses to small town dwellings. It didn't really matter to us where we lived, home was safe, fun, and full of love. My parents set an amazing example of what true love was and how to live content in any situation. Our entire family knew the value of hard work, and we lived by that principle daily.

I saw my Dad work 12–16 hours a day at the Tarong Power Station only to follow up with bible study and prayer meetings, and more work around the house. On top of all that, he would always find time for us kids. He never failed to play cricket in the backyard, go for a swim, take us fishing or teach us how to drive. If you ever wanted the best example of a servant-hearted, life-giving father, then look no further than my Dad.

Despite all the hard work, one thing that our family never really achieved or enjoyed was financial freedom. From a very early age, we lived in rented houses and enjoyed some truly remarkable homes in both Queensland and Victoria. Brand name clothes or shoes were considered a waste of money. Why would you spend $200 on a pair of shoes when you can get the same type of shoes for $30? In my younger years, a $50 pair of shoes would have been a significant investment. Why would you buy the fancy brands when you could create the look you wanted with much less? I still remember buying a green and gold tracksuit pretending to be a member of the Australian Olympic team, but even it only had two stripes, not three like the official Adidas version. As we grew and earned our own money, we were free to buy items of our choosing, but value for money was always a guiding consideration.

As a young boy, I formed some early foundational beliefs that would trip me up later in life. Built on the foundation of example and lived experience, I came to believe that nothing was for free. Before doing something fun in the afternoon, we had to work around the house in the morning. None of us had any problem with hard work; we loved it. And we could see that if we wanted to get ahead in life, we would have to work hard, perhaps harder than anyone else.

I would like to make one thing really clear. I do not blame my parents for anything. They did the very best with what they had, and they provided a loving home and a great family. We have strong relationships and still enjoy each other's company to this day.

However, many of the perceptions I took on as a young boy became the foundational beliefs that I have taken into mature adulthood. And to be completely honest, they became the cornerstone and strength of the CEO's internal operating system. Let me explain:

My internal perception of financial struggle helped shape my belief that I was born on the wrong side of the tracks. **My whole life would be driven by the desire to "get to the other side of the tracks".** One of my favourite movies is "A Knight's Tale" starring the late Heath Ledger. In the movie, the main character is a poor boy who leaves his father to live and work for a local knight. The father and son's shared dream is that this opportunity would help him "change his stars", or in my terms, get to the other side of the tracks. This desire became an unbelievably powerful internal driver for me, mostly subconscious and undisclosed, but very real and only now, 40 years later, very obvious. The CEO would use this as motivation to drive me to work harder, to work longer, to produce more, to be more, to achieve, to succeed… to get there.

In fact, this belief became so entrenched that it was the foundation of my addiction to work. You see, as time went on, it felt good to work. No, let me be honest, it felt great to work! It still does. I love working. If I have said it once, I've said it a thousand times. "I would work eight days a week if that were possible." Is there anything more fulfilling than getting paid to pursue your dreams, vision and calling? I don't think so. However, through my conversations with Virgil, I discovered that one of the trickiest things about workaholism is that it appears honourable, and it pays you. The harder you work, the more successful you become and the more it pays. Addiction often leads to financial and personal setbacks, while workaholism enables you to reap the rewards of your efforts and receive acknowledgment for going the extra mile. Wow, feel great and be acknowledged! Work became like jet fuel for the CEO.

## NO PAIN

Another early perception that became a foundational belief and strengthened the CEO was in relation to never showing pain. My Dad was a mechanic and worked on heavy machinery. Although completely non-mechanical, I loved to help him whenever I could. Inadvertently he would scrape knuckles, draw blood, and sometimes do some genuine damage. But never once did I see anything more than a slight grimace and an off-handed comment like… "Oh, better get a band aid." No injury ever stopped him from working, helping Mum or playing with us. Quite simply, nothing ever stopped him. One time, after I moved out of home, my Dad had a severe accident while working on my brother's motorbike. The accelerator cable became stuck on full throttle and Dad went flat out into some soft sand and a fence. His shattered leg required extensive surgery, and the doctors used an external fixator to help the bone regrow a full 10cm and return to normal. Dad had this fixator on his leg for about 12 months. On one visit just prior to my wedding in 1995, he changed a gear box in my Falcon Ute, fixator, and all. The rule of thumb was if there was no blood or bone sticking out, then just get on with it. Walk it off, it will be fine. Even if it is obvious and bad and you have a metal spring system sticking out of your leg, never, ever let the pain show. Don't let it beat you. This minor setback is nothing. It could be worse.

My brothers and I were in awe of this mental and physical toughness and as you may imagine, we all adopted this approach. We did our very best to never show or admit pain, no matter how much it hurt. When telling Mum about any incident or injury, we would always downplay the severity or paint a slightly more palatable picture of what really happened. If we were on the sporting field, no one would ever know that we were carrying an injury. One time, I did all the ligaments in my ankle while playing soccer for school sport. My ankle blew up like a balloon and I was struggling to walk. But I had an important game of squash that afternoon and was determined to play. I played the hardest person in my competition and beat them. Strange as it may sound, because of the pain I was not even aware that the game was over, let alone that I had won. Immediately following this, they took me up to the hospital and fixed a plaster cast on my lower leg. This cast meant that I would have to miss the swimming carnival at school the following day. The pool was about a kilometre from the school, so we all walked there in our house teams. Toughing it out on the way, determined not to show any pain, I gave my crutches to a friend and walked to the pool, cast and all. By the end of the day, this plaster cast was totally destroyed, and my ankle was a little sore. But no one ever knew.

This approach to pain of any kind is still with me to this day. Born out of my perception of what was good, right, and admirable, it had morphed into a foundational belief. Unfortunately, it's not a very good one; completely unrealistic and damaging to tell the truth. It is only now becoming apparent to me that not everyone thinks this way.

As you may have guessed, the CEO loved this belief. If you operate from a no pain mindset, you can never, ever be beaten. You might face some losses along the way, but you cannot lose. The CEO would use this to push me back to work and simply expect that I continue to produce more than before any injury. For example, if I had an injury that reduced mobility - of which there were a few - I could use the time in the office to get more work done. What an exceptional opportunity to do more work. And because I may have used some additional time getting around at work, I was free to bring some work home to set myself up for success the next day. I even used to boast about the time that I did a full stretcher night walk whilst on crutches. Hooray for me (just a bit deluded!).

My belief was that to show pain was to show weakness. And good leaders, good CEOs, don't do that. Yes, be vulnerable if you must, but don't let anyone know you are in pain. When the CEO combined this no pain philosophy with hard work and the internal drive to get to the other side of the tracks, well, let's just say, the increase in strength was akin to a bodybuilder on steroids.

## WIN / LOSE / WIN

Now, if you combine these early perceptions and foundational beliefs with working hard and never showing pain, then you can't lose. To be clear, it is ok to lose in a game. I have played competitive sport one way or another my whole life and I understand the reality of winning and losing. However, the real winning is in your mindset. If you learn from your mistakes, give everything you have, support your teammates, then you're a winner. The result of a game does not make you a winner or a loser. This is a mindset thing. The CEO used this mindset to add further strength to his habits and actions. Find a way to win, create a win/win scenario, do whatever it takes to succeed and do the best for everyone. In all honesty, I worked exceptionally hard to operate authentically and with integrity and to this day I do not believe that I ever used my position to win or get ahead by putting others down or setting myself up favourably.

However, the problem with a win/loss framework is everything becomes about winning and losing. Whether or not I like it, this framework ends with someone winning and someone losing. Remember, my internal beliefs were driven by the desire to get to the other side of the tracks. **I cannot lose! I must not lose!** If I lose, my entire future is in jeopardy. The CEO must win. Win with integrity and honesty and authenticity – but win.

## REAL MEN DON'T REST

I am exceptionally grateful for the model of my father. He is the epitome of a real man, and I have worked hard to follow his example and be the best man I can for my wife and my family. However, I have taken this noble concept and exercised it to the extreme. Regarding rest, I formed a very simple core belief: **Real men don't rest, they don't need to rest. To rest is a sign of weakness. If you rest, you are missing opportunities to produce stuff, to get stuff done, to be useful, to be productive.** Have a sleep in the middle of the day? You've got to be kidding. Do something. Anything. Connect with someone. Read a business book. Learn something. But have a sleep? What are you smoking? You've got rocks in your head. Ok, it might be reasonable on a holiday to have an afternoon nap, but come on, there are better things you can do with your time. Life is there to be lived. Live it to the full, you can sleep when you're dead. Normal people don't sleep in the middle of the day, and a CEO most definitely does not sleep in the middle of the day. That would be a complete waste of time.

## THE "SHOULDS" ARE STRONG WITH THIS ONE

My family loves the Star Wars saga. All my kids have light sabers and at least once a year we watch most of the movies in the series. As the story unfolds Chancellor Palpatine says to a young Anakin Skywalker that *"the Force is strong with you"* and Anakin pledges his allegiance and turns to the dark side, becoming the infamous Darth Vader. His desire for strength and power would lead him down a treacherous path in pursuit of what he thought was right.

As for me, the CEO's grip and ownership of my identity was gaining strength at a rapid rate of knots. These incredibly flawed internal beliefs were now acting in unison and feeding off each other. Not only was I a task-driven workaholic determined to get to the other side of the tracks, I was also a perfectionist who refused to rest or show any sign of discomfort, pain or weakness. I also had a very clear understanding of what I should be doing, and the CEO loved it. If I was to be successful, I really should do this, and this and this. The power of "the shoulds" became to me what the force was to Anakin, an insatiable drive and internal power that promised fulfilment and success.

This motive would appear everywhere and anywhere. For example, my daughter was playing a football carnival at Maroochydore on the Sunshine Coast. We were staying on the coast for the carnival, and I had taken my stand-up paddle board. After her games had finished, we were walking on the beach and I was keen to go out for a paddle, but the weather was terrible. It was windy, the waves were choppy and completely unsuitable for anything. There were no other surfers or paddle boarders out on the water, just a couple of kite surfers enjoying the wind and choppy conditions. However, I had made the effort of bringing my board all the way to the coast and spent about an hour arguing with myself about whether to take it out. In my head to win, I should take it out. If I didn't, I would have wasted all that time and effort and opportunity. I would have lost. By the way, I was exceptionally tired but had no capacity to give myself permission to have a rest. So, I took my board out. It was the worst paddle I had ever had. The wind was atrocious, the waves were worse, and the current was insane. After two attempts at catching a wave, I had drifted about 300m down the beach and would have to walk back with my 10ft paddle board against the wind. But hey, at least I tried right? Can't say I failed. Idiot!

## LIVE A LIFE OF PURPOSE AND FOR A PURPOSE: BE DELIBERATE

It's probably worth noting that not all my thoughts and beliefs are wrong or were wrong. Many are very healthy, and on their own, they can produce exceptionally positive results and admirable outcomes. It has been the combination of these thoughts and beliefs that have created the CEO's internal operating system and strengthened the fusion of my identity with the role of CEO.

For example, I gave my life to the Lord at four years of age and have always been determined to serve God to the very best of my ability. From the age of 10, I lived a very deliberate life. I knew I wanted to be a Physical Education teacher and did everything in my power to make that happen. Subject choices and good grades ensured I met the requirements to attend university. I succeeded in every area relating to this dream. Like many young people I had a few years of questionable living from the end of high school and into my time at university. However, my faith in Christ never wavered, and once I married Yvette, we committed our lives to serving and devoting ourselves to the Kingdom. Whilst at university I realised the incredible power of outdoor education and real-life experience. So, I said to myself that I would teach for five–ten years and then move into outdoor education, which is exactly what I did. I taught at a Christian College in Brisbane and the outdoor education centre I worked for was faith-based. Everything in my life came together. I was serving the Lord on a scale that was bigger than myself; I loved the mission, and the calling. The way we delivered programs from my perspective was the very essence of living out our faith. I was in control. I was choosing the direction of my life, and I was determined to succeed. As I received a promotion, I had the opportunity to serve the team and lead people from a faith perspective, making a genuine difference in the lives of tens of thousands of people every year.

The CEO's fusion with my identity was gaining strength. Even from a very early age, the CEO learned that hard work and good choices would one day see me promoted and successful. The more knowledge and wisdom I gained, the more positive the outcomes. When I didn't know something,

I worked hard to identify what I needed to know and to learn it well. My motive to be the best, or at least towards the front of the pack, grew stronger and stronger.

In 2013, I achieved fulfilment when the company officially promoted me to the role of CEO. After six years as a Physical Education teacher, and 10 years on the ground as an Outdoor Education facilitator, I was now given the title and role of who I knew I already was–the CEO. The fusion of this role with my personal identity was now complete. For the next 10 years, this fusion would only become stronger. Returning to the Star Wars analogy and the tragic tale of Anakin Skywalker becoming Darth Vader, this was me. Darren had become the CEO. And the CEO was hell-bent on winning, on being perfect, on success, on working hard, on being better than anyone and everyone else. The CEO had no time for rest and had no capacity for losing and the transition to the other side of the tracks was complete. Unfortunately, I had crossed the wrong tracks and now Darren ceased to exist. **The false identity of the CEO was my reality. I was the CEO.**

## REFLECTION

As a young boy, I internalised some very noble internal beliefs. Work hard, don't show pain, use your time and money wisely. They were not necessarily wrong, but it's probably worth asking the question that my psychologist asked me: Is it wise to let the little boy, the nine or 10-year-old Darren, dictate how I live as a mature adult in my mid to late 40's?

These beliefs were reinforced throughout my life, especially as I progressed professionally and in my early work years. They worked, until they didn't, which is partly why I am writing this book.

I invite you to pause and reflect on the following:

What is your attitude towards work?

What do you believe about rest?

What is your response to pain?

Are you competitive? Are you operating out of a win / loss mindset?

Write a list of your shoulds:

**What is your deepest internal driver? Where are you trying to get to? Who are you trying to be? What are you trying to achieve?** Moving beyond aspirational ideals here is difficult. Please resist the urge to say, think or write what you think you should, or what might be considered appropriate. We all operate from our deep inner core, and some of these internal beliefs are so ingrained and natural we don't even recognise them, let alone assess their validity. This work took me two and a half years to identify and process. And to be honest, even now I am challenged to keep them in check.

# CHAPTER 2

# FROM THE GROUND TO THE CEO

When I became CEO in 2013, I had actively worked alongside many of the staff either on the ground as a facilitator, or in close connection across the various roles required. I had worked with some staff for over 10 years and others I had hired, trained, and coached. To say that I was invested would be an understatement. As you may imagine, rising or being promoted through the ranks is not necessarily easy. Once a promotion is given or a title allocated, there is an immediate shift in relationship dynamics. Those whom you have worked side by side with for years now relate to you differently, even suspiciously. When you walk into a room conversation stops, or subtly shifts to other topics. You're no longer included in the *talk*, and it takes all the skill you've learnt and every bit of grace you have to rise to a new level of being, interacting and leading. Some people refer to leadership as a lonely place and I can attest to the fact that at times, I felt incredibly isolated. When you're working in the field, things are simpler, and problems appear easy to fix. Just ask any group of workers anywhere what's wrong with the country and what "they" (the government, or the council, or the leaders) should do about it. In fact, ask any group of workers what the boss should or should not do and you will get an extensive list of desired adjustments.

## POSITIVE LEADERSHIP LESSONS AND CREATING SAFETY

Now, some of the relational change is born out of insecurity or even jealousy. *Why did he get the promotion? That should have been me.* Some of the relational change is born out of assumption, true or false, it doesn't matter. Assumption doesn't require facts. It just requires a thought and a chemically charged emotional response. On one occasion, I asked the team to complete a questionnaire about their personal goals, focusing on where they saw themselves growing within the company. My only intent was for the wellbeing and positive future of the people I was leading. To achieve this, I asked them to outline some goals for one year, five years, and even 10 years. When I distributed this questionnaire, I explained to the team that I hoped to create a personalised career path for everyone in the company. I wanted to meet the team and everyone in it at their point of need, provide support and training and help them grow personally and professionally. Most responses were quite positive, simple, and direct. However, it was an eye-opener to me that not everyone thinks or lives with this kind of deliberate intention.

Further, some responses were incredibly confusing and honestly, a little concerning. Despite my well-presented rationale, several staff simply refused to answer the questionnaire. They responded with comments like, *"My personal goals are none of your business! Who do you think you are to ask me that?"* They often followed with probing questions such as, *"Are you not happy with me and the job I am doing? Are you saying you want me to leave?"* Insecurity and fear fueled these responses. I had been working directly with these people for years, sharing the highs and lows of life, including births, deaths, marriages and even divorces. Sometimes, I had even talked about these things personally, but because of the positional change in relationships, things were different now. People I had walked closely with for over a decade would now question my motives for action, change, and growth. The reality of this positional and relational change was difficult and sometimes painful to accept.

I have come to realise that fear is a primal motivation, and it produces a fight-or-flight response. The primal question is always "What does this mean for me?" And the fight-or-flight response can vary from every form of silence, including withdrawal, avoidance and masking through to violence, which may include name calling, labelling and attacking. However this fight-or-flight response is demonstrated, it takes skill, courage, and consistency to stay engaged and work through the challenges. The crucial conversations model for talking when the stakes are high became an invaluable resource for my leadership development here. (Grenny J, 2023). One challenge I faced in this leadership transition was to create a place of safety. People needed to know it was safe to engage with me as the person and as the leader. They needed to know the workplace was a safe place to be themselves, to grow, and even to make mistakes. In the early stages of my role as CEO, my leadership style was quite reactive and autocratic, which did not help create a safe environment. It would take a concerted effort on my part to adjust course here. *But more about this transition later.*

One revelation I had while leading the team was that everything I did and said was under constant surveillance. The team was watching everything to see if they could trust me as a person and as a leader. I might have said that I had their best interests in mind, but did I really mean it? Could they trust me when it really mattered? When push came to shove, would I create a safe place for them to work, to engage and to be their best? I would frequently face tests in public, in small groups, in large groups, and sometimes in the presence of guests or clients. For example, there were the gentle jibes from people who would see me in the office and later comment in the lunchroom that *"gee it would be nice to see you on the ground occasionally"*, or "*it must be nice to work in an air-conditioned office.*" While being gentle and genuine, I sometimes sensed that the comment carried an implicit message beyond its surface. Perhaps they thought I was losing touch. When I needed to follow up on an incident report or talk to a client about how their camp was going, the staff would watch to see if I would support them and their actions. They observed my interaction with clients and colleagues alike when addressing any areas of challenge. Over time, with consistency and gratitude, they learnt they could trust me. We created a positive culture in relation to all feedback and the team would even seek it out. Our clients responded exceptionally well as they knew we valued their input and would act immediately to adjust course if required.

Perhaps one of the strangest examples that dramatically increased the team's trust of me as the CEO and my leadership capacity occurred early in my role as CEO. We had a particular staff member who was genuinely gifted, although he tended to cross the line. Unfortunately, after many borderline incidents, a situation arose where I had no choice but to dismiss this employee. In the company's history, it was the first time we directly terminated someone's employment. As you may imagine, I was incredibly anxious and felt the full weight of responsibility relating to this decision. There would be the damage to personal relationships between myself and the staff member and there would be likely fallout between other staff as well. Further, we would be down a valuable person on the ground. However, in the end, it was a straightforward decision to make. I needed to act as the CEO on behalf of the company and our staff. The team needed to know that I would protect them and the organisation. I would keep their workplace safe. I would uphold the standards and values I was talking about even if it cost me personally and the company corporately. Ironically, after this decision, I had many staff thank me and indicate that if I had not acted, they would have had no option but to leave. They stayed because they could trust me, and they knew I would maintain a safe place for them to be.

These leadership lessons of modelling consistency, making the tough calls, and creating safety reinforced the CEO's core beliefs and I was developing a very clear sense of how I should behave and lead. It was important for the CEO to not only do the right thing, but to be seen to be doing the right thing.

## BELIEFS AND VALUES SHAPE OUR ACTIONS

This transition from the ground to the CEO was a genuine challenge and took several years. Although the title and responsibility shifted immediately, the size of our company meant I facilitated groups on the ground approximately 50% of the time for the first two to three years. It would take a lot of effort to completely "get off the tools" so to speak and focus solely on the role of being the CEO. In my typical style, I simply increased my internal and external expectations. I expected that my performance would be on par with that of a seasoned CEO, as well as a highly qualified and experienced facilitator. I wanted to show everyone that I was up to the task. Not only was I good on the ground, but I knew what was required to lead and grow the company. In these first few years, I worked in complete harmony with the CEO to prove to myself and to everyone else that I was the real deal. I was the CEO.

However, with every new challenge, success and achievement, a dark shadow of doubt was consistently present deep in my core. Subconsciously, I believed I was not good enough. I did not belong here. I felt like a fraud, an imposter. I was a fake. To succeed as the CEO, to pull off this illusion, I would need to not only work harder than everyone else but also to be seen to be working harder than anyone else. Additionally, the actual results would have to exceed everyone's expectations - mine, the staff's, the clients, and the company directors. I was simply prepared to do what was required to meet these expectations, and I also expected others to have the same level of commitment.

When it was time to upgrade the company car that came with the role in 2016, these flawed internal beliefs and associated emotions were amplified. The previous cars provided as part of my salary package were all considered by others as reasonable… a Colorado dual cab, a Mitsubishi Pajero, and a Nissan Pathfinder. However, this upgrade would be significant and draw many a comment from the staff. Because of the company being a not-for-profit organisation, we could get an excellent deal on a Land Rover Discovery 4. The final price was on par with a Toyota Prado; however, despite no one ever knowing the purchase price, the damage in perception was evident. This was a luxury vehicle that was well beyond me. The perception was that I was taking advantage of my position and that I didn't really deserve such a car. Believe me, this was not just a thought the staff had. I really struggled with this perception for a couple of years. Who was I to be driving a luxury car?

Fortunately, my diligent hard work, attention to detail, and leadership was proving beneficial. The company was growing year on year at a rate we had not previously experienced. We were increasing the number of weekly bookings for groups and hiring new staff. We were kicking some seriously good goals and even had to erect temporary tents to accommodate the overflow. During this time, we changed the company structure from an incorporated association to a company limited by guarantee with the express vision of expansion. I was actively leading on the ground and on the board of directors. We were seeking new members and new directors. Life was busy, life was challenging, life was rewarding and as the CEO, I was fulfilling my calling and leading the company exceptionally well.

Seriously, is there anything better than achieving your goals or exceeding them, growing personally and professionally, and building momentum towards a preferred future, with people you love and respect, in the service of an expansive God-given mission? Even working through the challenges of shaping culture and guiding people on a sometimes-awkward journey was proving very rewarding. I simply loved it. I would work as long as I could and try to be the best I could. It didn't even feel like work for me. This was just me, the CEO, doing my best. Or so I thought.

The truth is, the CEO's grip on my identity was gaining strength every day, with every achievement and with every challenge that I faced. I was not just responding as Darren, I was responding as Darren, the CEO. Driving to excel, to achieve, to win, Darren in perfect unison with the CEO would double down on effort, consistency and delivering results and it was working, the company was thriving, and we were kicking some amazing goals. I was not just learning how to lead. I was learning how to become the real deal - the CEO.

## 2ᴺᴰ GENERATION LEADERSHIP

Like many second-generation leaders, my leadership transition was challenging whether I was leading those below me in the hierarchy, or those directly above me. Our organisation was founded in 1996 and was transitioning from a family operation under the leadership of Bill, the founding director, into a very effective and mature organisation. I was the first leader of this transition. The weight of responsibility, sense of duty and obligation I felt toward the organisation was immense. I knew the ins and outs of the entire operation along with the internal and external motives, stories and beliefs that were driving the behaviours of individual team members. As a team, we were close and considered each other more of a family than colleagues. Perhaps unsurprisingly, not only did the team feel and act like a family, but several members of the team *were* family. We'd grown from one to two camps per week with five staff to approximately 35 staff delivering programs for up to 12 groups per week and almost 20,000 participants per year. Year on year growth had become the norm and the expectation. The rate of change and growth was accelerating. It was exciting and positive, and the CEO loved it. But, for many, the rate of change was excessive and fatiguing… it was too much.

The transition from the founding director to myself as the CEO was not without significant challenges. Bill was and is the very definition of an entrepreneurial visionary. Ideas and creativity were his thing. And mostly, these ideas were very successful and had created the opportunity for positive impact on thousands of people and for sustained business growth. However, as with many great visionaries, Bill's strengths were in creativity and starting things. Crossing the T's and dotting the I's were tasks to be done by others. His initial ideas, combined with his charisma and influence, drew people to him with a passion and desire to make things happen. Me included. My nickname for Bill was *"perpetual motion"*. He simply never stopped. Never turned off from the role. Many of us even witnessed that it was not uncommon for Bill to sleep in his uniform, so he was instantly ready the next day. Bill deeply loved the staff, and he showed his commitment to them by being extremely generous. This company was Bill's baby, his brainchild. Bill worked closely with Dave, Peter and Priscilla in the formation, early design and operations of the company and together they would invest heavily, laying the foundation for all future development. However, on a day to day basis, it was Bill who became the face of the company.

Since my promotion to the role of CEO in 2013, Bill had made and was continuing to make concerted efforts to step back and let me lead. We had developed quite a robust connection and could talk honestly and freely with each other. However, his level of influence and somewhat hidden role in the system would remain a constant challenge for me personally. Bill was the chair of the board and still owned a portion of the land on which the organisation operated. One must not underestimate the challenges intertwined in leadership transition. For the outgoing leader, particularly a foundational one, this is like watching your eldest child leave home, or perhaps giving your daughter away in marriage. The founder has given birth to this organisation, this dream. They have created every aspect of the operation, hired people to fill the roles, sought financial help and often invested huge portions of their own personal finance to make the dream happen. There will be no one in history as committed to the vision as the founding leader. This does not mean an organisation won't be better, grow and expand under the leadership of others. I am just identifying the truth that a foundational leader has a connection to the vision that goes beyond any other person. To let go of such a vision, or a dream, to let someone else pick it up and run with it must be terrifying. At this stage of an organisation's life cycle, fear is a driving force for the founding leader. The uncertain future of the dream they have created, under the leadership of others, is sometimes too much to bear. What if they do it differently? What if they don't quite understand how we do things? What if they drift away from the core mission? What if they have different beliefs? *What if they lose the heart? What if? What if? What if?*

When the founding director repeatedly expresses this fear to the incoming leader, it can be easily perceived as a lack of trust and even a vote of no confidence. **And this was my experience.** Despite our close, respectful, and robust connection, my relationship with the foundational leader, Bill, became more and more challenging. Again, I loved the vision, the organisation and Bill. I looked up to him as a mentor and role model. Our relationship had begun like a master and apprentice, grew into rabbi and disciple, and in some respects, almost felt as like a father and son. In my efforts to emulate Bill, I tried to follow his lead in storytelling, vision casting, and generosity. I even tried to copy his model of always being 'on'. I worked my backside off to impress him, and to refine what he had created and help it grow and thrive. After all, without Bill's vision, there would be no vision, no company, no role. I had found my calling in serving this vision and serving Bill. Together, we had navigated a change in company structure and were into our second strategic plan. We had travelled overseas with the team and led the organisation on a growth trajectory.

Unfortunately, towards the end of my time as CEO, there were several significant interactions and hurdles that created distance between us relationally. Bill did his job exceptionally well, as I did mine. However, when you navigate disagreement through tinted lenses and incorrect perceptions, damage is done. It did not matter how many times Bill said privately or in public that he believed in me and thought I was doing a better job than he ever did - hearing the words *'don't lose the heart'* repeated with compounding impact led me to conclude that Bill believed I already had. I couldn't just attribute this message to our disagreements, and I was unable to shift my perspective or belief about what he had said. I had lived and breathed this mission. My family had lived this vision with me. My entire identity had become intertwined with seeing the vision fulfilled. The message I heard and believed through my stained lenses of perception screamed loudly, "I don't trust you. You have failed."

**This was not Bill's fault** or even his reality. I know the man, and I know how he thinks. This was not what he wanted to convey. But it is what he said. My perception and reaction to this led me down a slippery slope of despair, disappointment, depression, and anxiety. I had failed. I was useless. I was not good enough. I was not enough.

The dark shadow of doubt in my capacity to be the CEO was being continually reinforced and it was almost impossible to conceive that my very best efforts were not enough. So, like all good CEOs who are workaholics, I just went to work and worked harder and longer and harder and longer. Surely, I could rectify things if I put in the time and effort, and others would witness this. Surely if I just worked a little harder, connected a little better, created something new, gave the team what they needed, created a better plan, produced a better report... surely, I would feel better. Surely, I would succeed? Surely, surely, surely.

## REFLECTION

**Leadership Lessons:**

1. Promotion and positional change can lead to isolation
2. Every action of a leader is closely observed
3. Motives will be challenged and questioned in private and in public
4. Respect is gained when you model consistency and authenticity
5. A critical role of a new leader is to create safety
6. Genuine beliefs and values will shape your actions
7. There will never be anyone as committed to a vision as a founder

As I had now fully fused with the role of CEO, my lens of perception became dull. I could not see the successes. The CEO acknowledged successes publicly, because this was the right thing to do, and it gave the team energy. However, no success was ever sufficient for the CEO. He took every perceived failure to heart, and as a result, I believed the story, the lie if you like, that I was a failure. The most significant damage was in the area of the most significant relationship, that was between me and the founding director. I had wrongfully placed Bill on a pedestal and tried to emulate him and see his vision realised and expanded. As a result, the words, "don't lose the heart" repeatedly expressed was like being stabbed in the heart with a dagger and I completely believed the lie that I was a failure. This led me to double-down and increase my effort in the vain hope that I could somehow change this perception through sheer will, determination, and hard work.

What lessons, good or bad, have you learned in your leadership so far?

How have incorrect assumptions, ill-founded or even unjust comments affected your sense of self-worth?

Is your identity fused with your role? What damage is this doing?

If you are a 2nd generation, or next generation leader, what challenges are you facing?

Are there any unhelpful comments that you have taken to heart? Are they true, or are they a lie? What do you really believe?

# CHAPTER 3

# PERSONAL GROWTH

As I began my leadership journey and my fusion with the role of the CEO, I knew very well that I did not yet possess the skills to do the job. I did not know what I did not know. After investigating a range of options, I made two significant decisions. The first was to enrol in a Master of Business Administration and the second was to seek guidance from an Executive Coach. Both actions were life giving and very rewarding. However, neither was without significant challenge.

Besides leading the company, I diligently completed my MBA one unit per semester over five and a half years. This included reading every night, doing assignments on weekends and public holidays and while on annual leave. I dedicated myself to producing the highest quality assessment pieces possible. I was driven to succeed at the highest level and applied almost everything I learnt immediately into the company. For example, because of the governance unit, I changed the structure of our company from an incorporated association to a company limited by guarantee. I began expanding the company's membership base to increase the number of directors and actively drove an increase in functionality and effective decision making. Because of the strategic management unit, I drove the new strategic plan and set in motion the course of the company that remains to this day. Because of the

HR unit, I reviewed all personnel contracts, updated them, and ensured that we were delivering the best possible packages for all staff. There was not one unit that was not immediately applicable to me or the company. I loved the work, the growth, and the opportunity to initiate so many positive changes.

With the CEO and Darren now beginning to drive the ship of personal growth in perfect harmony, I engaged George as an Executive Coach and would work closely with him for the next 10 years. This journey involved a few steps. We started with a DiSC personality assessment, which provided some valuable insight into how I saw and interacted with the world. It also empowered me to interact more effectively with my team. After a couple of years, I was excited about completing the Leadership Circle Profile - an exceptional tool designed to help leaders identify their reactive tendencies and to move towards operating from a creative mindset. The tool provided several ratings, including task/relationship balance, reactive/creative balance, and overall leadership effectiveness. In their own research, the creators Robert Anderson and William Adams identified that an organisation cannot grow beyond the capacity of its leadership. The 'data strongly suggests that if you can improve leadership effectiveness, you have a 38% probability of seeing that improvement translate into higher business performance' (Anderson R, 2016) (p14). Talk about motivation for a CEO to improve. I was ready and excited, and the result unexpectedly floored me.

Being a leader, someone who had worked with teams my whole life, a genuinely caring person full of vision and ideas, I thought I would rate reasonably with perhaps a few areas to improve. I expected a leadership effectiveness rating of around 65%, tweak a couple of things and be exceptional. However, the results of my first profile assessment revealed that my overall effectiveness was around 30%. Incredibly low, I was almost at the bottom of the leadership effectiveness scale. On top of that, it revealed that I was operating heavily from a reactive frame of mind, rooted in control. While

I showed some admirable qualities, my leadership style was autocratic, driven towards perfection and fueled by ambition. Much to my surprise, my lowest results were in relationships and self-awareness. Talk about some major blind spots and pride coming before a fall. Ouch!

So here I was driving change, growing the company, studying, and leading - all the while damaging relationships and reducing the capacity of others to follow my lead. This hit me like a ton of bricks, and for a while I was shocked and deeply, deeply disappointed.

Allow me to reiterate an important point here. My personal identity was now completely fused with the role of the CEO. There was no distinction or separation between the two. When I say, "I", at this point in time, Darren and the CEO are one and the same. The strengths of Darren were accelerating the CEO's growth and control and success. However, the losses were largely felt by Darren. The CEO did not like or respond well to any form of failure, but as would come to light later, Darren was paying the price. The CEO would simply push on at all costs. I was blissfully unaware of the cost of my approach on my family. From the CEO's perspective, this level of focus and devotion was simply required. It was exciting, challenging and rewarding. This was awesome. However, for Darren, this level of devotion came with a significant price tag. It cost time and relationships. Not only would I happily spend holidays, weekends and RDO's working on assignments, I would use it as an excuse to avoid deeper connections with our wider circle of friends. I must have responded to people as if on repeat, with comments like, *"Oh, that sounds like a great idea, but sorry I can't. I have to study,"* becoming an extremely common line for both my family and friends over this period. My wife and kids were incredibly supportive, but as my wife has said more recently, had she realised my motivations and hidden drivers back then she would have stood her ground and intervened. You see, I did all of this on my own time, alongside running the company full time. I was often working 50 to 60-hour weeks, and then studying on top of that. In simple terms, the CEO robbed Darren to pay himself. The CEO needed to work; to achieve; to succeed. The CEO's once noble motives and intentions were now hijacked by a long-time companion that would stop at nothing to be the best.

This companion was workaholism – what I call the Beast. It was born from my core belief in hard work and believe me, the Beast needs feeding.

## LEARNING MOMENTS AND A COMMITMENT TO GROWTH

Unfortunately, my story, perhaps not unlike yours, at times reflects exceptionally positive leadership, but is also peppered with examples of quite poor and potentially damaging leadership. One revelation I had very early on was that my growth was an intensely personal journey being played out externally for all to see, to feel, and to witness. You see, initially I thought I was a good leader. My motives were good. I was passionate about our mission and the purpose of the company. I was there for the team, but I did not realise how judgemental I was, or that I was operating out of a reactive mindset. My expectation was that people would deliver with the same level of drive and ambition that drove me when I wanted to get stuff done. I was so driven to succeed. Nothing would stop me. I once did a night walk on crutches because I had a broken bone in my foot. On other occasions, it was almost a competition to see who could stay the latest after a night activity or create the best connections or have the most significant impact on the group. I simply expected everyone to operate out of this type of mindset. It was a shock to me and not just a little frustrating when people started talking about work-life balance. As a leader trying to get things done, I absolutely hated this phrase. To me, it came across as an attitude that they want to be paid top dollar for doing less. This perceived attitude was in direct opposition to my internal beliefs, and felt almost insulting. To me, **work was life. Work meant perfect balance.** After all, you don't have to go to work if you are doing what you love and are called to do - right? As I grew into the role of CEO, this internal belief grew as if it were on steroids and as I would eventually discover, not everything that grows is healthy.

As I was operating out of a judgement mindset, my assumption was that people were judging everything I did or didn't do. Now, in part, this was true, but not always. For example, I assumed people were judging me for working in an air-conditioned office. So, I would go out of my way to connect with the staff during the day. To make this happen, I would put off some of my key responsibilities until later in the day and would happily work till 6 or 7pm with a sense of pride, especially if someone noticed the time when I left the office. Talk about a twisted pat on the back! But this would make me feel good. To work was good and helped me feel productive and important. I was doing what I was called to do. I would also frequently arrive as early as possible in the morning for the internal reward of being able to say to myself, 'look what I have done.' You can see the CEO and workaholic working in tandem here; The Beast-relentless in its desire to do more work; and the CEO-loving the results of the work.

Another example of my limited leadership capacity and the damage created occurred in the early stages of restructuring. My motivation was to include as many people in leadership as possible and create a system that would empower others to make operational decisions in real time. A good motive, yes - poor execution, even more so! A little unsure of what the structure should look like, I as a competent CEO, simply created a model and appointed people to the roles. At this time, we did not have an executive leadership team and all of these "new roles" had previously been my responsibility. So, I created our first leadership group with people assigned as Area Managers. The problem was, I did not provide enough clarity for each of these management roles, nor did I provide sufficient time for them to fulfil these roles on top of their existing priorities. I just expected that they would be like me and do the work on top of the work. Fair enough, I thought. Isn't that what leaders do? Shouldn't leaders be willing to go above and beyond what is expected? They do whatever is required to get the job done. Problems arose instantly and continued with incredible frequency. Worse still, the lack of clarity combined with the lack of progress and increased expectations inevitably resulted in good staff moving on; a loss felt by all, and not least by me.

Not one to enjoy failure, with George's help I engaged in the process and began the growth curve. I owned where I was and actively sought to address any area of deficiency, to improve first as a person, and then as a leader. As the CEO, I simply had to be better. I enjoyed this process, and the results although initially slow, showed genuine positive improvement. As you may imagine, I had some relational healing work to do, and this type of work takes time. I completed my second leadership circle profile in 2019 and was relieved to discover that my overall leadership effectiveness had increased to 65% and I was operating mostly from a creative mindset.

If you are a leader and want to grow, I highly recommend the Leadership Circle Profile. However, a word of caution. It is important that you are prepared for it. You must be prepared to face some hard truths. You will be required to dig into and expose some deeply ingrained beliefs, behaviours, and tendencies. And you need to be prepared to make some significant changes. This profile assessment is not for the fainthearted, but it is well worth the investment.

This personal journey, the growth and change within the company and the challenges of leadership transition were all happening concurrently. And while on one hand, the CEO's desire to win, to be better, to deliver better, to overachieve was so strong, and achieving exceptional results, I, Darren, was internalising any and every failure. Disappointment was prominent, and I was beginning to drown in depression.

I was judging myself for not knowing better, or leading better, or providing sufficient time and support for the staff to do their work. I did not realise that others also felt this judgement. My reactions were on display before I even realised that I had reacted. I found it quite easy to identify why things went wrong and who was to blame. Even if I didn't directly express blame towards others, people sensed it and found it difficult to meet my expectations. Truth be told, I could not live up to my own standards. After all, as the CEO, the buck stops with me. So, if there is fault, if there is responsibility to be taken, it is mine to take. This win/lose approach was simply unhealthy.

As you might imagine, there were many challenges to face and obstacles to overcome, but the CEO was up for the challenge. The rate of growth, change, and the push towards expansion generated a somewhat unexpected recoil within the team. While in any change effort there are always the early adaptors and culture carriers, I did not expect the level of resistance displayed from within the organisation, and the cracks showed up everywhere. You need to remember that I worked alongside many of these people since the early 2000's. If I had not worked with them directly, I had been personally responsible for employing them in more recent times and had worked hard to provide clarity with our future direction.

This unrestrained pursuit of growth, learning, exceptional productivity, and a desire to be a truly inspirational and transformational leader was taking a toll. I did not anticipate the level of interpersonal conflict and challenges in managing people. It also really took me by surprise that these challenges came from above, below, and sideways all at the same time. And on occasion, the level of abuse and blame directed towards me was deeply personal and incredibly hurtful. It was difficult to comprehend that some considered me to be directly responsible for their depression, anxiety, and stress. It was difficult to process that I had not provided sufficient clarity for people and that they suffered personally. And once again, it was heartbreaking to process that some believed I had caused this fantastic organisation to lose its heart. In their humble opinion and now in mine, I believed I had failed.

## AND THEN COVID HIT!

This was the most significant challenge any of us had ever faced. We were a thriving company and now, through no fault of our own, we were fighting for our very survival. We had to take an honest look at our finances and make plans estimating how long we might survive. In full survival mode, I worked with the accountant to create five different scenarios for the board to consider. This work included identifying who would stay, who would be let go and how much we could pay for how long. If you have ever had to rank your employees and prepare to end their employment, you will understand the depths of pain and anguish I was going through. Although not the scale of a major corporation such as an airline, with thousands of employees, planning to terminate the contracts of nearly the entire staff was the worst task I had ever undertaken. It made me sick to the back teeth. I felt like vomiting. In fact, even as I type this now, my stomach feels like it is being wrung out like a wet cloth. The stress and internal turmoil caused by this work was unparalleled with anything I had previously experienced. March 25th, 2020 was by far the worst day of my life. This was the day we stood our staff down and closed the doors. At this point in time, we had no idea if there was a future of any kind for the company and all we had worked for.

Covid was not the only factor that contributed to my downward spiral, but it was the catalyst that sent me into overdrive. There was nothing that could stop me from achieving or working my backside off to get the company going again. At this stage, I was in my element, facing impossible problems with a small but exceptional skeleton team, and all the passion of a dynamic leader. I was leading the way and running every tank dry. The work was not so much physical, but emotional. Every decision seemed laden with an additional layer of consequences and reality for me, the team and the company. It took me a long time to even notice what was going on and it took even longer to change my habits and behaviour. I could feel the stress and dissatisfaction rising. I knew I was not functioning well, but I could not put my finger on it or name it. And when I could identify the cause of a particular stress, tension or physical symptom, there was no way I was just going to accept it. In my opinion, this would have been a failure. Again! So, like a boxer fighting blind with one hand tied behind his back, I pushed on, still not knowing what I didn't know, but desperately searching and continually arguing with reality. This is what we call a blind spot. Something that is apparent to almost everyone else that we remain completely oblivious to.

## REFLECTION

**Leadership Lessons:**

1. Personal growth is an essential part of leadership and learning. Identifying what you don't know and how you will learn it is mission critical to effective leadership
2. Proverbs 4:7 states: "The beginning of wisdom is this: Get Wisdom; Though it cost all you have, get understanding"
   a. Pay the price
   b. Engage a mentor or a coach
   c. Do the study
   d. There is no shortcut to knowledge, wisdom and understanding
3. Learn the art of consultation and collaboration
4. Provide clarity

5. The pursuit of excellence, growth and learning are all good – but check your motives
6. Monitor the condition of your team and respond as required
7. Become aware of your blind spots and invite people to shine a light on them for you

This part of the journey caught me off guard. I sincerely believe that my intentions and actions were good and noble. I was not afraid to face reality. I was not afraid to grow, and I was not afraid to admit my mistakes, apologise and mature as a person and a leader. However, my insatiable desire and drive to succeed would strengthen the CEO's grip on my identity. The CEO was getting the acknowledgement for growth and positive change. Darren on the other hand, was internalising the failures. Publicly, the CEO was winning, but privately, Darren was spiralling into depression focusing on the failures and negative outcomes of the effective leadership decisions that had been made.

Are you aware of any areas where others perceive you to be winning, but you feel like you are failing, or have failed?

What are your blind spots?

Who do you have in your life who can speak with you directly and honestly? Do you have anyone to shine a light on your blind spots?

What don't you know?

What are you prepared to do about this?

How are others responding to your leadership style and interactions? Is there anything you need to change?

# CHAPTER 4

# BUILDING CULTURE

Building a positive culture from any starting point is hard work. In any organisation, there are patterns of behaviour that are truly exceptional. They are positive; they promote growth; they generate business and provide the team with a sense of value and purpose. The staff were committed to the mission. They had united in purpose and would work to support each other however they could. If someone was sick, another staff member would release them to go home and cover the load at their own expense. People genuinely cared about each other and invested in each other's lives, both at work and at home. When it came to delivering programs, everyone understood the importance of their specific role and worked to deliver the best experience ever. There was nothing that would prevent our staff from serving each other or the mission. Throughout my tenure as CEO, we had worked hard to collectively design and articulate why we existed and create the culture we desired.

## OWNERSHIP, SYSTEMS AND VALUES

One of the keys to success and outcomes achieved from building a healthy culture was taking extreme ownership. As the CEO, it was my responsibility to own the culture and to stop blaming others for the problems. As I type,

I am reminded of the scene in the movie "Remember the Titans" where the team is training badly, struggling with being the first ever mixed-race team. The whites won't protect the blacks and the blacks won't play for the whites. The white captain Gerry Bertier challenges his black counterpart Julius Campbell and tells him that his attitude is the worst he has ever seen. The young black captain simply, yet powerfully, responds, "Attitude reflects leadership… captain!" As the CEO, I realised that the fault or deficiency of our culture was my responsibility. If performance was lacking, training and development was insufficient. It was my responsibility to provide training and development. If time was being wasted, there was a need within the team that I had not noticed, and it was my responsibility to address it. If there was gossip, my communication lacked clarity and it was my responsibility to train the team in how to have conversations with the right people.

The second major initiative that contributed to building a healthy culture was identifying the systems that were operating within the organisation. The major system we discovered is encapsulated in the Karpman Drama Triangle, and is represented in the figure below.

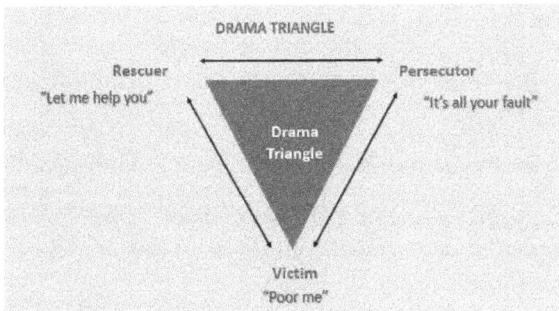

DRAMA TRIANGLE

Rescuer
"Let me help you"

Persecutor
"It's all your fault"

Drama Triangle

Victim
"Poor me"

**1. The Drama Triangle (Karpman Stephen, 1968)**

As the CEO, I realised I had been playing and operating out of this system for years and it was my responsibility to eliminate it from our culture. In this model or system, the three points of the triangle represent three distinct roles, the persecutor, the victim and the rescuer and these roles are played with predictable consistency. For example, as the CEO, I would create a procedure that would require a staff member to change their behaviour for the good of the whole team. This would make me, the CEO, the persecutor. The person asked to change would then assume the role of victim. Despite agreeing to the CEO in person, and even in writing, the victim would not want to change and would try to rally support from others. Discussions with others would go something like this: *"It's not fair, he has no clue. The way we were doing it was fine, this change is ridiculous."* The others in this scenario now become the rescuers. Seeing their friend and colleague distressed or upset, no matter how trivial the situation, invokes them to come to the victim's rescue. They operate out of empathy and take on the offense of the initial action. At this point the roles change. The victim and the persecutor then swap roles, and the original victim, now becomes the persecutor. They attack the original persecutor, who now becomes the victim, and the cycle continues. This system will destroy any organisation. It is truly vicious, fueled by gossip, assumption, half-truths, and innuendos. In this system, there are no winners. Not even the CEO!

If you can see this system in your workplace, you must address it immediately. The only solution is to step out of the system and own your part. If someone comes to you to talk about someone else, stop the conversation and direct them to have the conversation with the right person. Do not triangulate a problem. Learn the skill of talking directly and expecting others to do the same. **This is biblical and it works.** In Matthew's gospel we are reminded that this is the first step in the reconciliation process. Matthew 18:15 says: "If your brother or sister sins, go and point out their fault, just between the two of you. If they listen to you, you have won them over." In the following verses, provision is made to take others with you, but as a support and a witness, not to triangulate the grievance.

The final significant leadership action that helped build a healthy culture was to embody our values. The underlying premise is that values drive behaviour. If a value is not reflected in behaviour, then it is nothing more than words on a page or a wall. It became apparent that while we firmly believed in our values, our behaviour suggested otherwise. We had created a situation where it was difficult to talk to people, to raise issues and hold people accountable. Reacting out of fear, we would avoid correcting people or even requiring a higher standard of performance and this was doing significant damage. As CEO, I decided to lead by example and "walk the talk", which was one of our values, and we ensured that our actions, no matter how big or small, reflected what we believed. Everyone in the organisation was encouraged to do the same and positive examples of this were rewarded publicly and privately. When we addressed actions that were not in line with our values the response was almost always respectful, and the result was an enhanced positive culture and significantly strengthened personal relationships. Those on the receiving end would often thank the person for highlighting the area of concern. We were determined that our core values would not just be words on a wall. They would be a way of life. They would be the visible reflection of our culture.

## CARRYING THE BURDEN OF OFFENSE

As you may have realised, the CEO did not exist in the land of reality or balance. The CEO's way of operating was extreme. Hard work meant really hard work. Success and achievement were the result of this; there was no other way. However, the same extreme tendencies were evident when it came to taking positive action. The CEO would take ownership for everything. The motive again was good, but in the extreme, damaging. There was a significant gap emerging between the CEO's genuinely positive results and Darren's internal beliefs. Damage was being done and the pain of this culture building process was taking its toll. One of the problems with taking extreme ownership is our natural tendency to not only own the actions and outcomes, but to taking on the weight of offense, struggle, or lack as a sign of personal failure and this is what Darren was doing. Despite Darren, the CEO, successfully leading the organisation to a healthier position, Darren, the person, was internalising every fault as personal failure. I believed I had broad shoulders and thick skin. These problems were mine to own and to carry. These problems were my fault.

For example, when it came to dealing with the drama triangle the stress, fatigue, and offense carried by others landed firmly on my shoulders and once again I internalised these situations as my fault. I believed the comments that were made - I felt the grief of the offense caused and I could not escape the trauma affected by engaging in this system. This trauma was exacerbated by the fact that this company had begun as a family operation and many of the team members were actual family members. In fact, I had completely embraced this family team and felt the full weight of the "family response" that could often be volatile and unrelenting. Challenges to any one individual were often perceived as an attack on the entire family and sadly, I would receive a gentle word of caution from another family member, sometimes even from Bill, the founding director. The problem was these people were my friends; they were my family. These types of responses cut me to the core and led me to believe once again that I had failed them - I had failed the family... I was a failure.

Perhaps naively, I did not anticipate the negative fallout caused by leading and living our values. Because of this focus on values, we could begin creating a learning culture. We moved away from judgement and accountability towards learning and growth. We considered the staff able to grow and learn and to take responsibility for themselves. The buy-in and the positive change in culture were next level, and it continues to build in this manner today. However, this was hard work and as the CEO, I had taken several body-blows through this process. Not everything went smoothly or according to plan. One error of judgement and lack of investigation almost lead to an unfair dismissal claim. I faced the music of this action at a "special board meeting" and felt as though I had lost the confidence of the board, or at least a couple of key players. Yes, one of them was **Bill**, the founding director. This situation revealed an internal belief of many within the company; **If someone leaves, it is the fault of the leadership.** And to be fair, many of these people moved on because of actions that I was responsible for. On the back of leading by values, expansion, new directions and COVID, the company had experienced significant staff movement with more than a 50% turnover rate in the past 2.5 years. This movement included direct family members of the founding director and people who had been part of the team for between 15–20 years. **These changes were not insignificant. It felt like we were losing family members. These people were my friends. Once again, I internalised these losses as failures. I had let the company down. I had let my friends down, I had let myself down, I had failed.**

As you read this chapter, you could be forgiven for thinking that the CEO was not the problem. In fact, the CEO's leadership and the subsequent outcomes were incredibly positive personally, professionally, and corporately. However, there was a subtle development beginning to emerge. Darren, the CEO, was firing on all cylinders and prepared to do the hard work and make the tough decisions and build a healthy culture. But it was Darren the person – me, who was internalising the negative outcomes of these actions. I took on the full weight of blame and persecution from others and fully believed the lies, the criticism, and the fact that people had moved on because of me. To use a sporting analogy, the CEO was kicking goals, and I was the ball. The internal damage to Darren was becoming extreme. The CEO was winning the battle for my identity and Darren was dying little by little every day. Something had to change!

---

# REFLECTION

Leadership Lessons:

- **Three keys to building a health culture**
  a. **Ownership**
     i. Lead from the front
     ii. Lead by example
     iii. Model consistency
  b. **Identify the systems operating within the organisation and make the necessary adjustments**
     i. The Drama (Victim) Triangle is extremely damaging
     ii. Own your part in it
     iii. Stop engaging with it
     iv. Train your people how to have the challenging conversations
  c. **Lead by your values**
     a. Values must drive behaviour
     b. Talk about them, train them, do them
     c. Reward those who consistently demonstrate them

- **Do not let the responses of others affect your core**
  a. You are not good or bad based on the opinions, comments, and actions of others
  b. Your value is not dependent on the opinions, comments, and actions of others

---

How about you? Are you kicking goals on one hand, but taking on the lies and offense and burdens of others as personal failure?

The only way to reduce the gap and the pain is to accept reality. Yes own what is yours to own, but be gentle with yourself. You are not a superhero. You are human. You have feelings, it does not matter how thick your skin is or how broad your shoulders are, you are not meant to carry other people's offenses or problems.

What can you let go of today?

## *Journal Entries October 2020 – December 2021*

### *October 2020 - Current Situation:*

- *High pressure–self-perception / self-inflicted*
- *High stress–actual physical tightness in chest*
- *Really don't want to admit or acknowledge this pain*
- *Not listening to my own advice*
- *Lack of self-care–Just an intense desire to meet my own very high expectations*
  - *Still trying to perform and achieve more than anyone else*
  - *Still seeking validation / acceptance through performance*
    - *Compounded by events of the year and board responses*
    - *Have to work even harder to prove worth and value*
    - *Very low motivation to do what I know is good for me – e.g. exercise / eating well*
- *Finding it difficult to give myself permission to invest time in self*
  - *Self-care is very low*
  - *Self-leadership is therefore very low*

**Result:**

- *Grind*
- *Task*
- *Do*
- *Produce*
- *Fatigue*
- *Lack of effectiveness*
- *Fairly unproductive – which is the opposite of what I am trying to achieve*
- *Limited fulfillment*
- *Others don't see joy / inspiration*
  - *They see stress, fatigue, pressure, etc.*

**Insight:**

- *If I cannot give myself permission to stop and reflect and invest into my growth and leadership, I cannot increase my capacity and therefore won't be able to release them into their best place of leadership*
- *A team cannot perform beyond the capacity of its leadership*
- *I am either the greatest increasing factor or the greatest limiting factor*

*Why am I so task driven?*

*Why do I need to achieve? And be perfect? And be better than everyone else?*

- *Trying to fulfill prophecy*
- *Doing all that I can*
- *Fear of failure to deliver on this*
- *Value is coming from what I do and what I achieve*

*Perception:*

- *I am a grasshopper in own eyes*

*The subconscious voices relentlessly yelling in my head:*

- *Who am I?*
- *Who do you think you are?*
- *You don't have a national profile*
- *You don't even connect with those in your area!*
- *Who do you know?*
- *You don't even have any money*
- *Why would you be used to change the nation?*
- *You haven't got a clue*
- *You don't know what you are doing!*
- *You come from the wrong side of the tracks*

*Insight:*

- *Fair bit of fear driving my thoughts and behaviour*
- *Playing not to lose–again*
  - *Not telling Yvette*
  - *Not doing anything either more positive, or even more negative, just staying in ordinary*

*How do I get past the shoulds?*

- *Increase curiosity*

*November 2020*

*Stress in chest all day…*

*Preparing for board meetings appears to be a bit of a trigger*

***Very disappointed with my efforts** for Remembrance Day… no sound, no microphone…adjusted well but this should have been better*

*Poor choices on my part not to act when I first thought about it a couple of weeks ago*

***5th March, 2021***

*Incredibly flat*

*No drive*

*Really feeling under the weight of it*

*Struggling to name "it"*

*Internal story:*

*Who the hell am I?*

*Severe internal block to actively grow and promote the company… pick up the phone!!!!*

*Very tired all the time… even when going to bed early, just not waking up refreshed*

*Really feeling the emotional load of people leaving... even the ones that needed to go*

**This is a question of me and my identity?** *Theoretically, I know it is not, but...*

*Not completing any tasks, just playing at the edge of what I should be doing*

*Great support, but feeling really isolated professionally and personally*

*Trying to give myself permission to take a week off, but what would I do to justify the time and be better than I am now?*

*Session with George – (Executive Coach)*

*Part of role is to create the opportunity out of the struggle*

*Storm is on the inside*

*Take the pressure off and have some fun*

*Find connections to move forward*

**15th March, 2021**

*What a few weeks*

*Three staff resigning... good result? Yes!*

*A great relief and physical shift in demeanour once decision made*

*Leadership discussions... We were able to get past the emotion and only deal with what we know... We did not and have not made assumptions and were able to find a relational win/win path forward albeit uncomfortable*

Need to manage staff morale as at least one more announcement imminent

Praying for the right staff to join us

### 15th June, 2021 Reflections:

- Pain in chest has returned
- I have a board meeting this week
- I am not sure if it is related or stress by association, but really feeling the stress at the moment
- I have come back from my break reasonably refreshed—much better than I was
- I am mostly thinking clearer, but it is apparent that I do not have a large tank of capacity
- I am finding myself struggling the longer the day goes on
- I have noticed today that I am avoiding excessive interaction with clients and people in general and have really felt the stress today
- Have thought long and hard about ringing a psychologist. I have his number
- Had the phone in my hand ready to go, could not / did not call
  - I think this is a fear response
  - Fear of judgement, being less than a capable person – a clear sign that I do not have it all together
  - Why am I trying to protect myself? – This might be an underlying question of pride?
- In my head, I know it is the smart and the right thing to do – I would encourage and support others, but to be honest, I am really struggling to take the step and make the call

- ○ *After all, I'm not going that bad, not bad at all really, this is just normal stress and I am more than able to handle the situation(s), I just need to do the jobs in front of me, pretty simple really*

### 21st June, 2021

- *Another resignation … actually a good thing, could see some genuine culture challenges with this person continuing*
- *My chest hurts and sense of personal value and worth taking another hit*
- *Even with the announcement of this latest resignation, the vibe of the group is incredible*

### 4th July, 2021

*I am finding it hard to focus on any one thing and to get anything of use done.*

*Being a task driven perfectionist, this is not a good feeling. On a personal level, I have hit an obstacle that feels overwhelming and to be honest, I dislike the idea of confronting it.*

*In one sense, I know this is largely a matter of perspective, but my emotional tank, my energy tank, my resilience, and grit building tank along with all the energy that I have had previously are below empty.*

*I have taken time off work (two weeks at the start of the term) and by the end of the term I was already tanking. I am again on two weeks annual leave, but to be honest, I'm a little concerned that I am not putting enough in the tank to prepare me for what lies ahead.*

*I have gone to see the doctor and need to establish a mental health plan – **this is not something people like me need**! There is no blood, no bone sticking out*

– no outward sign of injury or reason for substandard performance or output. I do not find any of this easy to talk about. It is incredibly hard to articulate things in my mind, let alone share my thoughts with others. So, when people talk about the stigma of mental health, I have come to realise that it does not come from others; it comes from within. Then, if I feel that way about myself, the automatic assumption is that others also think that way.

The battle is in the mind - the most strategic place in the world; *'As a man thinks in his heart, so he is'* (Proverbs 23:7 NKJ). So, in some ways, it makes sense to see someone who can help with my mind, how I think, how I process things, how I see myself and others, and how I measure success.

Yvette has been an incredible help, the perfect wife, non-judgemental, my biggest supporter and gentle. She is really encouraging and has stepped up to carry the load. Unfortunately, this is taking a toll on her – it is not her responsibility to carry my load. It is a genuine privilege to have such a wonderful wife. I know she is always there for me. I have an obligation to get things sorted.

**One of my challenges is to align what I believe in my head and even my heart and match that with what I have lived.** I, 100% believe in God and his word and his promises but have really struggled to lead a full life. In what I have read in the scriptures and learned over the years. Perhaps I have some misunderstandings and need to readjust my perspective, my thinking, and my convictions. Of particular frustration is my financial situation.

It is difficult to understand how I can manage the finances of a multimillion-dollar organisation but struggle to run my budget and grow the funds to get a deposit for a house.

*18th October, 2021*

*"What the hell is going on?*

*I had a very easy day yesterday, went to church, had coffee, and caught up with friends. I saw my mum and dad and chose to have a sleep in the daytime, instead of playing basketball. I even watched a movie and went to bed early. I felt totally smashed before going to bed and yet once I was there, I could not sleep and have woken today feeling worse than I did when I went to bed. Made it halfway through the day and went home, nothing in the tank. This is really ticking me off! I am tired and want to sleep but really struggling to give myself permission, because that is not a good use of time, that is not how men use their time. I really want to dig in and get to the bottom of the story(s), but have no real idea of what I am doing. To be honest, I just want it all to go away. I want to be normal and feel good and capable, not to mention "productive!"*

*19th October, 2021*

*The shoulds are very strong with me and I would like to understand the internal stories and rules that I am listening to, the ones that are driving my behaviour. In my head, I need to be the best, lead the best, produce the best, deliver the best.*

*I am somewhat of a perfectionist and I am very driven…. Why and to what end???*

*Work*

*In my head, I must work hard. This is what men do. This is how you become and remain successful. Not working is simply not an option. Work is a privilege. I love to work. I can't just not work!*

## Rest

I do not rest well - if at all. Rest is a sign of weakness… Keep working and get stuff done. I struggle to understand God's concept of rest and entering his rest. I kind of get it in my head but have a massive amount of trouble actioning this. It is so hard to take a day off or rest – especially when I don't produce something.

## Achievement / accomplishment / getting stuff done

This appears to be where I get my value from—doing stuff. And doing stuff to a really high standard. Get it done, get it done right, get it done on time or early. This is probably not a really healthy thing to pass on to my kids – it probably sets them up for failure. Don't waste time, effort, money. Use every opportunity - get the most out of every occasion.

## Real Men deliver

They produce. They work hard. They achieve. They provide. They win. They lead. They inspire others.

The sense of failure story

Wrong side of the tracks story / change your stars

If I can work hard enough, I will get there… or will I? Is it even possible? Is it just a pipe dream?

## Success measured in:

Making it (whatever **it** may be). Crossing the tracks – changing status. Comparison with others. Possessions, house / land, car, title, position, financial *freedom / security. Clearly this is wrong and not entirely in line with what I say I believe, but it is probably where I am at currently.*

### What is the current story?

- *One trigger was the special board meeting… I think I took the board's response as a "vote of no confidence!"*
- *Relationships were damaged – particularly between Bill and myself! This damage and distance remains*
- *I have worked my backside off trying to prove myself. Where what was once understood and given, I now have to prove again, and again*

### What do I really believe about God?

*Personal Saviour! King of the universe! Interested in me! Gives my whole life purpose! These thoughts override the thoughts below, although not all the time. Sometimes, they may be more aspirational desires than core beliefs… I choose to believe anyway – which I think is the essence of faith. I am struggling to see the fullness of God play out in my life and lived experience. I know I am speaking from my own limited perspective here.*

*"I come to give life and life to the full" (John 10:10) … "Give and it will be given back to you pressed down, shaken together and running over" (Luke 6:38) … "I have plans for you, to prosper you and not to harm you" (Jeremiah 19:11)… "Test me in this" (Malachi 3:10) – regarding finance. **I think despite my best reasoning and understanding, I have viewed God in terms of the prosperity doctrine. Although I have given willingly and cheerfully, I have probably given with a hope of some kind of positive return, as if God is the great bank in the sky** – after all he owns the cattle on a thousand hills, and aren't we heirs of the whole estate? My motives have been*

wrong! I come with my wish list and hope that he will provide. When this has not occurred in the way I would like it to happen, the internal assumption is that there must be something wrong with me … perhaps I am not good enough, not worthy, not valuable.

My position in life results from my own decisions and please believe me, I am not trying to apportion blame. I think God is less concerned with my financial position than I am. **This translates, in my mind, to the assumption that God is not interested in me. I simply know this statement is a load of rubbish, but …**

I don't think God is vindictive, however, if I am being honest, I view God as an external, judgemental God and not necessarily a loving father who desires a relationship with his chosen ones. There seems to be a significant distance between me and Jesus Christ, the Holy Spirit, and God the Father. I have never really had a close relationship in this space. When I remember asking for the gift of tongues, it felt like the gift was only for others. I am grateful for the word I have now although, I would like to be more aware and in tune with the Spirit – just not sure how. My reading is all over the place. I probably don't listen very well – I know he is speaking all the time. I am disappointed in the lack of favour in prayer, especially for Sam's healing - but that is another story.

**25th October, 2021**

**Slightly agitated all day. So hard accepting feeling bad all the time. Chest hurts today. Mind all over the place.** Boys helped clean, sweep and fold clothes. All that is good, so what the hell is going on? Why can't I just embrace where I am, relax, enjoy something… anything? My habit is to find something to do and just keep doing it… some of it useful, some of it not.

# PART 2

........................................................................

# BURNOUT AND BATTLE SCARS

# CHAPTER 5

# WARNING SIGNS

A s you can see from my journal entries I was really struggling towards the end of 2020, and this continued to escalate throughout 2021. Every day I had an unrelenting burn in my chest, an anxiety of sorts, and a sense of impending doom that I knew I would be responsible for. Daily as I drove into work, my chest would go into overdrive and the closer I got, the slower I drove. My chest would feel heavy and burn at the same time. Anyone in leadership would understand the potential of dealing with some sort of incident or interaction daily. For me, I knew this feeling well and the CEO led me to believe that it was a positive thing – almost a CEO's superpower in the form of an early warning system. This was just normal and expected. We had set up a working structure that released me to do the work of a CEO; you know - strategic planning, vision casting, connecting with guests and clients, etc. Our structure ensured that others covered the daily tasks. I did not have to worry. But I was the CEO, and I felt the full weight of final responsibility for everything; interactions, incidents, decisions, and even outcomes. Despite very few of my fears and assumptions ever being realised, this daily load was getting heavier. I could usually hide these feelings from staff by pretending I was totally interested in everything happening as I drove in. They had no idea I was struggling. The CEO became exceptionally gifted at hiding emotions and fears. Protecting the image of the competent CEO was mission critical. Whatever you do, do not let anyone see that you are struggling, or don't have the answers, or don't have it all together.

Because of the Covid-19 pandemic, our strategic plan was 12–18 months behind schedule. We also had some significant capital works to do on the property to meet a range of council requirements. This had put a significant dent in our expansion plans. Another delay. Argh! In the past few years, we had experienced a staff transition rate of approximately 50%; a level never experienced in over 20 years of operation. Not all of this was bad. In fact, as an organisation we needed some staff movement. Sometimes we welcomed it, but more often, we did not. But as anyone in leadership would know, the work of offloading established staff, onboarding new staff and creating a positive culture is a mentally and physically draining experience. As Jim Collins summarised in his classic book "Good to Great", getting the wrong people off the bus and the right people on the bus, and in the right seats is one of the most critical roles of leadership (Collins, 2001). However, let me make it clear, this is much easier said than done. Culturally, we were really kicking some fantastic goals and yet I could not escape the burden on my mind and my heart of releasing good people for whatever reason. I knew we were doing things well, and we were learning with every interaction, but many of these people were my friends and to see them move on simply hurt. On top of this, as the ever-growing CEO, I was working to be authentic, vulnerable, and relational. The unspoken sense of letting people down, or people feeling that they had no option but to choose to leave, magnified my sense of loss and failure.

If I drove into work slowly, worried about some impending doom, then my drive home was worse. I would drive out even slower with an increasing sense of failure and disappointment. In my head, I was the CEO. I should have been able to anticipate these challenges and potentially address them before people left. Perhaps if I had led the team better, they would have jumped on board and stayed. Perhaps they would have grown too. But as the old saying goes, "You can lead a horse to water, but you cannot make it drink." The harsh reality of leadership, adult growth, and learning is that the responsibility lies with each individual. If someone does not have a desire to grow, learn or change, they won't.

The battle for my identity was intensifying. The problem was that I did not even realise who or what I was fighting. The CEO knew, and he was living the dream and hell bent on winning. But as Darren I was just failing, and I honestly believed that I was a failure. Good people had left, and more were leaving. We were behind schedule, with no concrete plans in place for expansion. **My mental state was in freefall, and pain was coming…**

## VISIBLE SIGNS

The reality of living completely fused to the role of CEO was becoming more visible daily. At this point in time, I was experiencing an intense burning sensation and tightness in my chest every day. It never really went away. I felt genuinely stressed all the time. I would often rub my sternum to try and push it down and suppress the feeling. This never worked. I had no interest in looking after myself, investing in time for myself and my motivation for anything remotely positive outside of work was non-existent. I was almost always disappointed in myself, my actions and especially my poor use of time at work. It didn't really matter what I accomplished on any given day, no degree of success or achievement was satisfactory. I was not sleeping well at all. If I went to bed before 10pm, I would still be awake at 2am. If I went to bed after 10pm, I would wake at some ungodly hour and not get back to sleep for at least two – three hours. It was a good night if I managed three – four hours sleep. Fatigue was a constant but unwelcome companion and I felt incredibly flat all the time. I had no physical energy and no drive. I could not identify what was going on or why, so I would often just sit in my nothing box, pretending I was ok and have a glass of wine. At night, despite being desperate for sleep, I would procrastinate for as long as possible, because I knew that going to sleep would just accelerate the arrival of tomorrow and I was already struggling. My productivity was severely tanking. Not only was I struggling to concentrate and make decisions, I could put things off for hours, just barely trying to justify my existence but, I was actively avoiding people - staff, clients, friends, everyone and was feeling less and less passionate about what I was doing.

At this point in time, I knew I was completely absorbed with the CEO role, but to be honest, I did not see this as a problem. I was just being true to who I thought I was, the CEO. I was not aware that there was a battle raging for my soul, my true self, my identity. I just thought this was normal stress and fatigue associated with the role. Something to be expected and handled. Isn't that what good leaders, and competent CEOs do?

In October 2020, I had watched a Global Leadership Summit presentation by Carey Nieuwhof, where he talked about the causes and signs of burnout. Because of his own journey and research, he said that burnout often results from situations where you have high responsibility mixed with low control and low results. Hello! This sounds familiar. He identified 11 signs that might be indicators of burnout. Individually, these signs may not be that significant, but in combination, the effect can be deadly. These signs included: your passion fading; not feeling highs or lows; disproportionate reactions; everybody draining you; you're growing cynical; nothing satisfies you; you can't think straight or logically; your productivity is tanking; you are self-medicating; rest and sleep don't refuel you; and you don't laugh anymore. At first, I thought to myself, this is interesting, I think I'm pinging on about four of these. But later that night, when I looked over my notes and spent some time in honest reflection, I came to realise I was pinging on all 11. This was not good. I knew I was in serious trouble. He had just described my reality.

A few months later in April 2021, the company's Executive Leadership Team, Jack, Anthony and I joined some other like-minded leaders on a whitewater canoe trip on the Clarence River in northern New South Wales. We had a blast navigating through some challenging rapids and falling in more times that we would care to admit. Sitting around the campfire on the last night, we were enjoying a glass of "milk", (read whiskey), discussing the company and how we were each travelling. It was during this conversation that I first shared with anyone how I was feeling and what was going on behind the scenes. The guys were quite surprised but extremely supportive. It was a small measure of relief to get some of the weight off my chest. However, for self-preservation I remained very closed and cautious with how much I shared.

This moment of sharing lead me to take a couple of weeks leave with the hope of a quick reboot for the rest of the year. The CEO's mindset here was very simple. Get back to work. Sure, take a couple of weeks off, refresh, reset and get back to work. Plan your return if you like and do reduced hours if you need. But get back to work. The CEO's primary motive was simple: get back to work! And his internal belief system said, "If I have to go through burnout, then I am going to kick its butt."

This was the pivotal moment that led me to seek professional help and meeting Virgil on the 25th August 2021 and as I mentioned earlier, things got a lot worse before there was any sign of them getting better.

## 2. Clarence River: Where I first shared with Jack and Anthony that things weren't going so well

I tried multiple times to return to work from this point forward. I would take some accrued annual leave in the June/July holidays and another week in September. Reluctantly, I agreed to take some anti-depressant medication at this time. To me, this was a major sign of failure. Unfortunately, when you reach the point that I had, your body exhausts all the natural chemical reserves that assist you in managing difficult situations. Even if the chemicals are produced, the body depletes them quickly due to insufficient quantities. As my doctor would later explain, the purpose of the anti-depressant medication is to help rebuild a satisfactory baseline of these important chemicals. But again, my "no pain, no gain" story working in cahoots with the CEO ensured my acceptance of taking any medication did not come without a significant reading of the failure story. I wasn't allowed to complain as my wife wouldn't allow it. They were the rules apparently!

Although at work, on site and present, I was grinding through the day to day and was largely unproductive in the back end of 2021. The CEO had the whip out and demanded that I get back to work. Push, push, push. He was unrelenting. The problem was, the harder I pushed, the weaker I became. I totally believed every lie the CEO was selling. In my mind, I was a failure. I was not being a real man. I was wasting time, effort, and money. I couldn't afford to rest. So, I dismissed all indicators saying otherwise.

I had many sessions with Virgil during this time and it was in November that he provided reality check number two. After listening to my story as if it were stuck on repeat, he turned to me and said directly, "**You are an addict. Darren, you are a workaholic.**" Thanks Virgil! Ouch! That stung a little. "Am not!" was my amazingly mature internal response. "I'm not an addict, I just love working. What's wrong with that? Fair crack of the whip mate, I don't steal, I don't cheat, I'm not taking drugs, I'm not a burden on society. I'm a contributor. I am the real deal. I am the CEO." Obviously, I did not say this to Virgil out loud and chose to politely go along with his outrageous assessment. Unfortunately, he was right. He would explain that the problem with this addiction is that it pays you, whereas other addictions are visibly toxic and destructive.

Society applauds workaholism as noble and often compensates it well. However, the truth remains, like all addictions, left unchecked, it will kill you. The CEO was in some sickly twisted way, quite proud of this diagnosis and used it as fuel to drive me on… after all, if I am a workaholic, then that is just who I am, not my fault. Let's get on with it. I would refer to the workaholism almost as another separate identity. I called it the Beast.

However, my mental state was in freefall, and not even the Beast was winning. I now dreaded going to work. I would drive in slowly. My walk became a trudge and my passion had almost completely evaporated. I would do anything to avoid people, colleagues, clients, and participants. Sure, I would go out to be seen but would keep my distance and if there were any interactions, I would keep them short and succinct, never allowing myself to get drawn into a discussion of any interest. I would bury myself in some sort of work in the office, which was clearly of the utmost importance. But then, in the middle of that work, my productivity was tanking. I was not productive and decision making was beyond me. I could sit for up to an hour just trying to make a simple decision. And please don't let the phone ring or require me to make a call. I could not think straight or logically. In fact, my mind was so foggy I could barely think at all. I was simply filling in time until I could justify leaving. My greatest challenge was trying to convince myself and pretending to others that I had done enough for the day. I even commented to a staff member once that a good day for me was when I printed something out. This is a truly embarrassing admission. *I was the CEO of a multi-million-dollar organisation and the best I could do was print something out – it didn't even have to be good. This was my sad reality.*

## REFLECTION
**Leadership Lessons:**

- Ignoring or suppressing physical symptoms is … stupid
- The weight of leadership responsibility is easier to carry when it is shared – you were designed to work with others
- Being honest with yourself is the first step in creating awareness
- Find some people in your corner who you can trust and confide in – a team, a coach or mentor
- If you find yourself protecting something – an image, a belief, a perception, check your story and the true motive behind this need for protection

Time for some honest reflection. Are you struggling with any of the warning signs identified in the story so far?

If so, circle the ones below that you are currently experiencing or have experienced in the recent past.

- Your passion fading
- Not feeling highs or lows
- Disproportionate reactions
- Everybody draining you
- You're growing cynical
- Nothing satisfies you
- You can't think straight or logically
- Your productivity is tanking
- You are self-medicating
- Rest and sleep don't refuel you
- You don't laugh anymore (Nieuhof, 2018)

Who can you talk to about this? Set up a meeting and talk it out now. Do not delay. Have the courage to share honestly with them and with yourself.

Invite them to be honest and share any observations they may have made about you and your recent actions/behaviour.

Now that you have identified some areas of concern, what action steps will you take today?

If you only circled a couple of these warning signs and you are happy with your current actions, please stop immediately and check your story. Challenge what you are believing. I would argue that experiencing any one of these warning signs is a major red flag that requires urgent attention. Initially I believed my story that I was ok, these feelings were just normal and should be expected. I couldn't have been more wrong. Please don't make the same mistake. Take action now.

If you didn't circle any of these warning signs, I am truly relieved, but I would ask you to consider if there are any signs in your life that might indicate you need to make some adjustments. Write these below and identify what you will do about them.

# CHAPTER 6

# DAMAGE DONE

## BURNOUT

Things were not looking good at the start of 2022. I had my usual long Christmas break and returned for in-service training. I loved this time with the staff, setting the course for the year, sharing vision, inspiring the team, and leading. My message in 2022 was kind of ironic. I had taken a photo whilst at a lookout on a bush walk. From this lookout on a clear day, you can see hundreds of kilometres from the Great Dividing Range all the way to Brisbane. But on this day, there was nothing more than rain and a thick fog. In fact, you couldn't see more than a few metres, and a sign that read: '*A window to a changing world*'. On the back of Covid and burnout, nothing could have captured the situation more aptly.

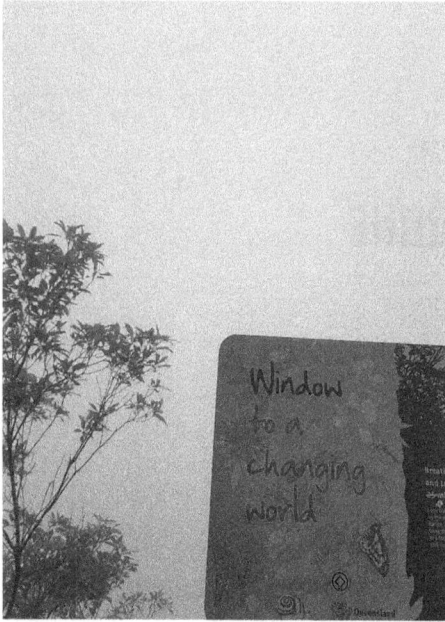

## 3. Window to a changing world

At the beginning of February, I was looking forward to a meeting I had scheduled in Tasmania. Knowing the effort required to get through the first few weeks of the year, my thought process was to give everything and then have a break in Tasmania after this scheduled meeting. This would allow me to come back refreshed for the rest of the year. Not a bad plan, in my humble opinion. We had a full week scheduled for our in-service program. On the 4th day I could not make it past lunch. I was completely out of batteries and was near breaking point. I was emotional and unstable, so after quite a degree of internal struggle and mental gymnastics, I went home. The following week I lasted only three days before having another moment and going home. I would end up taking the rest of January off on sick leave, returning for the Tassie trip in early February. The meeting in Tasmania went well and my time away was special. But as you may have guessed, not enough. ***Be aware, if you find your emotions are all over the place and your energy levels rapidly deplete despite good rest, you may need to make some significant adjustments now.***

On my return I lasted about a week. In true CEO form, I decided to review my performance against the KPIs of the strategic plan. Now remember that Covid had significantly smashed the company around, and dented our overall outcomes, but I was the CEO. So, I just went about adding the current year's KPIs to those that were not met from the previous year. Here's that old familiar story again – do more, do better, get it done, just work harder, you can do it. The Beast was in overdrive. The CEO had zero sense of reality, and even less compassion for a body and mind that was fading. Just get yourself into gear and get it done. Wow, talk about crashing and burning. Things were now getting really serious. I had no option but to write a letter to the board requesting to take the rest of the term off with a view to return after Easter. I knew I had significant sick leave up my sleeve, and I was running out of alternative options. The board approved the leave, and I took a break. However, my motive had not changed one bit. Get well, so you can get back to work. I had no other thought process. Just do whatever it takes to get well, to heal, so you can get back to work and lead. The CEO was still firmly driving. He was happy to take time off. He had earned it and could justify it. But the motive was not about just getting well. It was about getting well, to get back. But I had a very long way to go.

These nine weeks were exhausting and frustrating to say the least. I was consumed with doing the work of dealing with my crap and getting back. I was fully committed to this process and this outcome, but my mind and body had other ideas. My reflection from the 15th February 2022, captures my situation well. At this time, I was living the reality that I was once a competent and passionate CEO who now couldn't get past 9am without wanting to go back to bed. The only sensation I had was numbness, as if I were struggling through a slimy pit of mud, with no visibility of its magnitude or the path ahead. I was breathing, just. It was like trying to stand on my tiptoes gulping for breath like a goldfish out of water. Not only that, but the cat was also now out of the bag, people knew the truth and I felt vulnerable, exposed, and insecure.

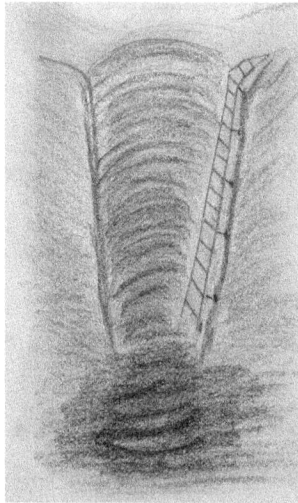

**4. The Pit**

*15th February, 2022*

*I have decided to take extended leave - nine weeks. I really hope that this is enough time. I know I need to take this time off, but to be honest, I feel like I am conceding defeat. The picture in my head has me hanging off the bottom rung of a ladder in a seemingly never-ending funnel-like pit.*

*I know the importance of changing my language and imagery, but I am just trying to explain how I feel and where I am. Acceptance sucks. Losing the fight sucks. Not knowing how to win sucks. Being indecisive sucks. Feeling dreadful and in constant turmoil sucks. Being disappointed in myself sucks. Not being able to trust my physical or mental self sucks. Listening to the negative voices in my head sucks. Sitting watching TV sucks. Doing nothing sucks. Sitting here processing a mountain of rubbish sucks. I am sick of this!*

*Who am I if my job gets taken away from me? Where has this insecurity come from?*

Sleep continued to be elusive. Almost as soon as I went to bed, my mind would race with all the things that had to be done and how I should or could go about achieving them. Even if I had the luxury of dreaming, it would be about work, and I was consistently waking up more and more tired. To make matters worse, I would use procrastination and self-medication as an avoidance strategy. Flicking channels and having another glass of wine became the norm. Boring and potentially harmful, but the norm. Truthfully, I did not really want to go to sleep because I knew that the sooner I went to sleep, the sooner I would have to face tomorrow. There is a level of pain and anxiety that comes with dreading tomorrow and I could not escape it.

When tomorrow came, the battle was on instantly. The first and immediate daily challenge probably sounds really stupid now that I write it down; **what will I wear today?** I remember sitting on the stool at the end of my bed for about half an hour trying to decide between wearing shoes or thongs. Seriously! Who cares? Obviously, me, the CEO. Image was very important for him. The way I dressed affected every interaction and what others might think of me. Yes, even when I was at home resting, trying to work through everything - how I presented myself to others was my priority. Struggle if you must, but don't let anyone see it.

Let me be honest here, the physical, mental, social, and spiritual outworking of burnout is intense, and embarrassing and it bleeds into every area of your life. You are in it. You cannot go around it, or over it, or just choose to avoid it. You have no choice but to go through it. There is no map, no instruction manual, no compass, nothing! Worse still, the first session with Virgil was just the beginning. For me, things became a lot worse before there were any signs of improvement.

At the time of writing, I have been seeing Virgil regularly for almost three years and we have been working through a particular model called ACT or Acceptance and Commitment Therapy. A prominent Australian psychologist, Russ Harris, developed this model which focuses on accepting reality, whether it is good, bad, or otherwise, without judgement. You cannot change it, so just accept it, and then commit to a course of action in line with your beliefs and values. I have found this model quite beneficial. It has not been looking to appoint blame or to try some clever three step avoidance strategy or pretending things aren't as they are. This model has helped me to identify and deal with reality. Albeit really slowly.

However, the problem with any psychological model, or medical model for that matter, is that the first step is to create awareness and awareness can lead to further challenges. For example, when you go to a doctor, he or she will ask a thousand questions to identify the symptoms and create an awareness of the cause. Only after gaining awareness can anyone suggest a path of positive action or prescribe medication. Psychology is no different. Skillful questioning, intentional listening, and honest reflection lead to awareness. Unfortunately, awareness leads to a sense of exposure and the results often include an increase in symptoms, triggering a downward spiral.

Let me explain my situation. The generic assessment tool for mental health is your DASS score. That is Depression, Anxiety and Stress Score. These three factors usually work in unison. It is common to be high in one area and low in the others. My initial assessment showed medium to high stress, medium depression, and low anxiety. However, my newfound awareness would lead me towards significantly increased depression and later increased anxiety. In fact, the doctor's official diagnosis was that I was suffering from a major depressive disorder.

I had to face and accept some harsh realities, but I did not want to. So, I fought and fought and fought, thinking foolishly that I could win. **Remember, the CEO is in the driver's seat, and he is hellbent on getting back to work.** He was determined to go through burnout better and faster than anyone else. The CEO saw this as a new challenge - some kind of twistedly exciting new goal that he could achieve in a condensed time frame. Not only would I go through it, but I would be better for it, and so would the company. Please believe me here. I am not making this up. This was my genuine train of thought and reflected my core beliefs. I was hard wired to win at all costs. Sadly, with every fight, I became weaker and weaker and more damaged. More depressed, more fatigued, more lost.

Let me share some realities that came to light and just how hard I fought against them rather than accepting them...

I was physically exhausted and had completely run out of batteries. Unable to hide from reality, I had become a shell of my former self. Incapable of working or engaging in any physical activity for longer than a few minutes without being totally shattered for the next few days. The fatigue was intense and debilitating. My eyes would sink so far into the back of my skull that I was looking like the emperor from Star Wars. They were so dark that the first time my psychologist saw them, he thought I had two black eyes and asked if I had been in a fight. "Sadly, no," I replied.

"This is just me!" He would come to use them as a gauge for how I was travelling. Every time I walked into his office; he would awkwardly stare at my face to see how I was really going. It was no use trying to hide my state of reality. My eyes would tell a damning story.

I had no interest or capacity to engage socially, whether it be going to church, hanging with family, or having dinner with friends. In fact, I would avoid these situations at all costs. I hated being in any crowd. If I went to the shops or out for coffee, I would always sit in a quiet, dark corner with my back to the wall. I needed to see out and be able to get to the exit quickly and, 'please, God, don't let me come across anyone I know!' I became an expert at flipping a conversation away from myself or anything personal and moving away within a matter of seconds. This would often come across quite rude and left my wife or kids to cover for me and explain. They were very gracious. I remember one time in church - I had deliberately arrived late and made my way to the back corner of the raised seating whilst the music was playing. I was pretty sure no one saw me enter. As the service went on, I noticed several people, friends, in the few rows directly in front of me. They had seen me during the service, (damn it) and I was desperate to avoid any interaction with anyone. As the speaker was drawing his message to a close, the anxiety burned intensely in my chest. My rate of breathing rapidly increased and I felt exceedingly agitated. I was fidgeting in my seat and physically looking for the fastest escape route, knowing that I would have to go past these people. As soon as the last song began, I simply said to Yvette, "I have to go." I got up and walked out, not looking to the right or the left. I just got out as soon as I could and went to the car. Ahh safety! Please hear me, social anxiety can be terrifying. It makes little sense, but it is real and can be debilitating. I would not wish it on anyone. If you struggle in these social settings and find yourself looking for a way out, please seek some help.

As the burnout advanced, I had zero capacity for anything new. No new learning and no desire for personal growth. I could not focus on reading, and to be honest, I had no genuine desire to. Where I would once love to digest a new business book or read a story that might enhance my leadership capacity, my passion and purpose had completely vanished. I just couldn't be bothered. And besides, the fatigue caused by that sort of concentration was not worth the effort.

And spiritually, well, let's just be honest here, I felt depleted and dry, essentially dead. My reading was haphazard and shallow, almost non-existent. My relationship with God was distant. An ideal, but not a life-giving reality. Just another thing I had failed at. In fact, I felt disappointed, angry, and frustrated with God. After all these years of faithful service, where had it gotten me? My prayers were like wishful "bless me" shopping lists and I was questioning everything I believed. This was an unsettling time.

## BATTLE SCARS

It was only now, as my awareness was increasing, that I realised I was in a fight. The CEO knew, and he was winning. He was fighting hard and dirty. He was using every trick in the book, and I just kept playing into his hands.

For example, I struggled to accept that I was indeed a middle-aged man, suffering burnout and that I had been diagnosed with a major depressive disorder. All reports and advice indicated that recovery was not guaranteed and that it would take quite some time. Now first, what is a middle-aged man? I intend to live to 100 or more, so I suppose when I turn 50 this could be true. However, in my mind I still envision myself at my peak capacity and believe I should be regarded as the athlete I was in my mid-thirties. Accepting that I was fatter, slower, less coordinated, and needed more time to recover was incredibly difficult. In fact, it was not something that I really wanted to believe at all. This happens to other people. Not me! I am the

CEO. I am in control of all things, including my physical state and rate of decline. Second, I was struggling and tired, yes, but major depressive disorder? **Mmmm? What a joke!** Again, as I write this down, you must be thinking that I am some kind of deluded idiot. But before you judge me too harshly, how are you going with this?

However, during this time off, despite constantly swinging between fight and flight mode, I managed to spend some serious time seeking wisdom and direction from the Lord. On one occasion, I felt led to ask what he wanted me to let go of, and his reply was instant. **Fear and control!** Processing this, I realised I was genuinely afraid of losing face, being irrelevant, not being able to do my role and even losing my job. In defence, I had been trying to control everything - my image and reputation, my capacity, my financial position, and my standard of living. I followed the Lord's advice and saw him wrap these in a leather-bound scroll and take them with him to the cross. I saw a vivid picture of Jesus on the cross with the word 'pride' tattooed on his forearm, and my scroll of fear and control bound in his hand. He was telling me plainly that he had already paid the price for my sin and my pain. All that was required of me was to let go and rest in him. This was a special moment for me, and I did my best to follow his lead.

**5. Jesus taking my fear and control**

However, as you may have guessed, I struggled both mentally and phys-ically. The fatigue after this session was incredibly intense and I felt like I was back at ground zero. My mind was extremely quick to play its own tune and question any positive thought process or forward movement. Cynical questions and mocking comments flowed through my mind like a raging river - unstoppable and damaging. What if you aren't ready to return? What are you even doing? Others are better at your job anyway. You're just wast-ing time - you're useless - you're cooked!

## BUT WAIT THERE'S MORE...

A few days later, I went for a ride on my mountain bike at Mt Peel, a small reserve with bush walking and mountain bike tracks. Yvette was home, sick with vertigo and I was doing my best to restore my mental and physical health. Jesus had been speaking to me clearly and for the first time in a long time, I was listening. His most recent direction was to not rush and just be. This made no sense at all and did not line up with my core belief that rest was a sign of weakness. So, in my foolish lack of understanding, I asked the Lord to continue speaking to me and invited him to be blunt and direct if necessary.

I was enjoying the ride and was on the last track on the way home. **Perhaps the name of the track is quite apt: Gumbi Gumbi.** As I came over a small rise, my front wheel hit some soft dirt on the edge of the track. Next thing, my face was slamming into the ground, and my body arched backward like a scorpion over the top. I don't think I have taken such a large hit before. Still conscious, but badly winded, I checked to see if everything was still working. The instant pain was a dead giveaway that something was not quite right. After regaining a small sense of composure, I took a couple of photos, got back on my bike, rode back to the car, and drove home. Yvette got quite the fright when I entered the bedroom with dirt and blood all over my face and laboured breathing. **Long story short, after a shower I went to the emergency department for scans which revealed a fracture of T5 and compression between T6 and T8.** Praise God, the pain medication soon took effect, and I could breathe easier, although my back and neck were quite stiff.

**6. My bike, my face and the X-ray**

Now I know God has a sense of humour, but I had not even made it half-way down the track before I ate dirt; talk about blunt and direct. One thing I have learned, or am at least beginning to learn, is that when God speaks, you should probably listen, and perhaps avoid asking him to be blunt and direct – ask for gentle.

Fast forward to the end of term, and you guessed it, I was not ready to return and needed more time. The Board were showing some additional signs of concern. Perhaps they had missed something? They asked for formal medical reports from the doctor and the psychologist. These reports did not read very well, and the CEO was not overly happy. The result was a graduated return to work under strict conditions. Virgil was very direct in his instruction, saying that "Whatever Darren thinks he can do, reduce it by at least 30%, even up to 50%." Whatever! My comments to the Executive were fairly direct; *"What on earth do you think I have been doing? I have been working to get back. I have literally focused on nothing other than getting better."* Don't you hate it when others can see a better picture of reality than you can? The CEO was driving hard and determined to get back. Darren at this stage, although having gained some increased awareness, was not fighting against the CEO. He was fighting for him. Darren was still completely fused with this false identity. Due to my extended absence, the Board promoted Jack to the role of acting CEO. Fair enough, it was only short term. *I will be back before you know it, just wait, and see.*

The restricted return to work plan was to start with 10 hours a week and increase to 15, and then over time, move towards 25 and even 30 hours a week. The plan was to be full time and back in the saddle by the start of term three. In true CEO style, I wrote the plan and set about achieving it. I even created an accountability spreadsheet where I would closely monitor my time and pat myself on the back for going home as ordered. Things were good. ***"I was winning again"*** thought the CEO. How is this for a classic example of the CEO's drive? In the first week of the return-to-work plan, I did 13 hours and followed up with 18 hours in the second week. And I felt great. *I'll show you what I am capable of. Reduce my expectation by 30%, whatever!* Perhaps predictably, I hit rock bottom harder and faster than ever before after this effort and felt like I was all the way back at square one. The fatigue smacked so hard that I felt like a boxer being given a standing eight count stupidly trying to show the referee that I was ok and ready to continue the fight. But hey, I was determined; I had just had an extended break, and I had just written a plan to get myself back to full-time work. You can't stop me now!

Throughout Term 3, I followed the plan diligently and steadily increased my hours. It did not really matter to me how I was feeling, or even how productive I was. I was there, and I could stay a little longer and push a little harder. Despite my best efforts, the most I could consistently deliver was about 25 hours a week. This did not stop me from trying to do more, but the result was always the same, a rapid depletion of all reserves. Severe fatigue, increased depression and now an increasing level of anxiety. I was beginning to worry about my reducing bank of sick leave.

In all this time, the company continued to thrive and kick some amazing goals, but I felt no joy. I did not feel any highs or any lows. At our quarterly financial and Board meetings, I would feign enthusiasm and excitement. I had the facts to prove just how well we were going and what was possible, but I felt nothing. No joy, no excitement, no sense of satisfaction. Just show me what is next. Can you understand what I am saying? We were doing record sales and increasing capacity at every level. Morale was good. Finances were good, the future was good. But to me, nothing! I felt about as excited as someone on the way to a funeral of some distant lost relative who I hardly knew.

It's also worth mentioning that my return to work was not entirely seamless. I felt really displaced. The Acting CEO, Jack, had been working out of my office in my absence and would have to move out again, eventually. I was working hard not to step on his toes, but **I was still the real CEO!** Jack had been doing a great job without me, but I knew stuff. I could do stuff. People were excited to see me back at work, but as usual, I kept my responses safe and seldom shared a deeper understanding of my ever-present reality. To add a level of complexity, an expansion opportunity presented itself and my task would be to create a business plan for the Board to consider. Yes, I was steering the ship again – sort of!

During this period, my sessions with Virgil were consistent and reasonably intense. To be honest, just knowing that a session was coming up triggered a heightened sense of anxiety. This was also true in the lead up to Board meetings. The level of concern from the Board was also increasing and Chris, the chair of the Board, had asked me to consider not returning to the role of CEO until I returned from my upcoming long service leave in the middle of 2023. *Mmmm! Ok, what's really going on here?*

Perhaps one of the most useful revelations in my psychology sessions was a very simple equation, Virgil would talk about the concept of suffering. He explained in simple terms, the greater the distance between your expectations and reality, the more you suffer. And I was really suffering.

## EXPECTATION − REALITY = SUFFERING

Virgil, an avid golfer, used the analogy of a golfer stuck in the trees. Now, they have just missed a 50-metre-wide fairway, but still think they can split a one-metre gap between two trees while chipping over the sand trap and land on the green just inches short of the hole. Being reasonable at most sports, I could fully understand this analogy. In fact, I don't think it would surprise you to know that I have tried that exact shot so many times. After all, trees are 90% air anyway. Like the foolish golfer, I was still not making the required adjustments. I was still hellbent on returning to work. I had no other picture, no other plan. Get well, get back. Be the CEO and lead the company into the future.

Talk about battle scars! I felt fatigued, stressed, depressed, and my anxiety was growing. The Board was incredibly concerned and began to waiver in their confidence that I could return. My Executive colleagues were concerned with my lack of progress. They cared deeply, but at my request, they could also deliver the brutal truth. Typically, I was ok with this level of honesty. It had been a hallmark of our Executive relationship. However, in my weakened state, a couple of comments hit harder than expected. Jack once said that he was "sad that I was going through this so poorly." He had no other intention but to express his personal concern about how hard the journey was for me so far. But you guessed it, I took that as judgement. In the eyes of one of my closest colleagues, I was now failing at recovery. Anthony had been a longtime friend both in and out of work. In fact, I had the privilege of both hiring and promoting him to the Executive. He was also now asking some challenging questions, the most confronting of which was, *"What if you don't make it back?"* **Are you for real?** It felt like I was lying wounded on the battlefield in extreme pain with dislocated limbs, broken bones, severe bruising, exposed jagged abrasions and blood pulsing out from open wounds. Instead of telling me everything would be alright, their comments seemed to scream, **"Oh mate, I don't think you're going to make it."**

But the battle wasn't over yet.

## THE MOUNTING CASE AGAINST THE CEO

The stories that shape our core beliefs often establish themselves in our early childhood, and they help us make sense of the world. Even as adults, they remain powerful drivers for how we interact with the world. They help us succeed. They help us know the difference between right and wrong, and they help guide our decisions in work, in love and life. As I have shared, it was these stories that became the cornerstone of the CEO's identity and strength. I measured every interaction in my life through these stories and they reinforced what I believed without question. Some of the CEO's beliefs, values and behaviours were excellent and well intentioned. The damage was done when these became fused with my identity, and I lost all sense of myself outside of this role. I would now argue that living our adult lives with the perspective and understanding of a child is reasonably foolish. The devastating impact on Darren was on display for all to see.

## 7 Impact of Fused Identity

| Stories and Core Beliefs | Resultant Actions | Fusion of Identity with Role of CEO | Impact / Outcome for Darren |
|---|---|---|---|
| **Getting to the other side of the tracks** | Absolute, insatiable drive to succeed and achieve | Destination focused<br>The future was always on the line<br>Darren cannot fail, must not fail | Failure<br>Never satisfied |
| **Hard work** | Task driven perfectionism<br>Projects and finances ahead of budget<br>Increased capacity to do more | Work became the means and the end – just keep working<br>Diminishing satisfaction | Excessively intense fatigue<br>No physical or mental capacity<br>Failure |
| **No Pain** | Never stopping<br>No acknowledgement of personal need<br>No investment in personal health<br>No self-compassion | All warning signs ignored<br>Pain, stress, depression, anxiety just normal – push on | Physically and mentally spent<br>Constant Pain in chest<br>Major depression<br>Increasing anxiety<br>Leaning on alcohol |

| Win / lose / Win | Do what must be done – with integrity<br>Do not fail | The future was always on the line<br>Darren cannot fail, must not fail | Failure<br>No rest<br>Fatigue |
|---|---|---|---|
| **Real men don't rest** | Do not stop<br>Never rest<br>Push on | Fatigue was something to fight against<br>Fatigue was not real or acceptable | Extreme fatigue<br>Sleeping in the middle of every day<br>No energy for anything<br>Total physical depletion<br>Total mental breakdown |
| **The shoulds** | Figure out what you should do and do it better<br>Be more, do more, achieve more | The list of shoulds increased with compounding impact<br>I could never achieve success, or satisfaction | Reinforced failure<br>Nothing satisfied<br>No achievement or action was enough |

| Live a life for a purpose and on purpose: Be deliberate | Fully embrace the vision and the mission This comes first at the expense of all reason, personal health, family, and social relationships | Full fusion in mission, vision, role, and identity Nothing else mattered Darren did not exist outside of this purpose | Total loss of passion, care and eventually commitment The only focus was work |
|---|---|---|---|

With this fusion of identity, there was no reason for Darren to exist. If Darren was not able to kill the false identity of the CEO, he would literally cease to exist. If Darren continued to live out of this false identity and these inaccurate stories, he would die. If he did not die physically, he would almost certainly live the rest of his life as a pathetic shadow of who he was meant to be. The CEO on the other hand did not care, as long as he was driving and working and succeeding, it did not matter at all what happened to Darren.

## REFLECTION

### Leadership Lessons

- A truth shared in a soft, gentle, or kind manner is better than brutal honesty
- Every degree of separation or distance provides greater perspective – trust those who can see a different or bigger picture
- Expectation – Reality = Suffering
  - Do whatever you can to reduce the gap
- Always challenge the stories you are believing
- You are more than your role

It took me a long time to acknowledge and accept the physical symptoms I was experiencing. I was the CEO and thought that this level of stress was normal and expected.

There were several physical indicators that eventually gained enough of my attention to cause me to seek help and find myself sitting on a psychologist's couch. Until I took the time for some honest reflection, I was living in denial and my health was in free fall. In the list below are some of the major indicators I experienced.

Do any of these apply to you? If so, circle them:

| | | |
|---|---|---|
| Stress | Elevated heart rate | Inability to |
| Anxiety | Chest pain | concentrate |
| Depression | Fatigue | Inability to make |
| Disappointment | Burning sensations | decisions |
| Lack of joy or | Feeling of heaviness | Diminished |
| satisfaction | | productivity |
| | | Poor Diet |
| | | Lack of Exercise |

In our fast-paced, high-performance world, it is normal to have two or three of these indicators at any given time. However, if you are experiencing high levels of any of these or think you might be "pinging" on a number of them, the time to act is now. See someone you trust, perhaps your pastor, a counsellor, a doctor, or a psychologist. I had to fight every internal voice in my head to make it ok to seek help, but praise God, I won that fight. I would hate to see what might have happened if I did not seek professional assistance.

What is your view of work? Do you love to work? Do you enjoy staying longer than others?

Are you a perfectionist? Are you driven? Where did this start?

Do you have a healthy work/life balance? What would others say about your approach and relationship with work?

What is your attitude towards pain?

Does the win/lose framework influence the way you interact with others?

Do you live your life deliberately and for a purpose? Is this purpose legitimate or has it become all-consuming?

What is your attitude to rest? Do you actively take time to disengage, or do you prefer to be "always on"?

I have found that operating from a "should" motive is extremely damaging for me. Are there any beliefs, behaviours or habits that are motivated by what you think you "should" be doing? Is this "should" accurate or valid? What adjustments may be required?

## CONSIDER THE SUFFERING SCORE EQUATION:

**Expectation – Reality = Suffering**

Are there any areas in your life where there may be a significant gap between your expectations and reality? Use your own ratings from 1–10 (1 being the lowest or worst, and 10 being the highest or best), to identify your suffering score in each of the following areas. If possible, identify any adjustments you could make:

### 8. Suffering Score – Personal Evaluation

| | Expectation | Reality | Suffering Score | Adjustment Required |
|---|---|---|---|---|
| **Productivity** | | | | |
| **Achievement of Goals** | | | | |
| **Relationships at work** | | | | |
| **Relationships at home** | | | | |
| **Physical fitness** | | | | |
| **Social interactions** | | | | |
| **Spiritual habits and growth** | | | | |
| **Personal and professional growth** | | | | |

## INSIGHTS:

Take a moment to think about yourself and your own identity. Who are you? What makes you unique? What are your dreams, goals, core values and beliefs? What do you love? What do you hate? What are your deep internal drivers?

Now also take the time to think about your role(s) at work and home. It is logical that there is similarity, however can you identify any areas where your identity may have become fused with your role(s)?

For example: Finish this sentence:

I am _____

If you answered by identifying a role, then you may have fused your identity or a portion of it with your role.

For example:

- I am a teacher
- I am a coach
- I am a lawyer
- I am a doctor
- I am a pastor
- I am a CEO / COO / CFO
- I am an accountant

Similarly, if you answered by identifying a task or skill, you may have fused or partially fused your identity with this task or skill.

For example:

- I am good/not good at problem solving
- I am good/not good with numbers

- I am good/not good with people
- I am good/not good with technology and social media

Every example above is a description of a role, or skills involved in performing those roles. It is likely that you do fulfill these roles, perform these skills, and execute these tasks extremely well. However, let me be clear:

**You are not your role. You are not your skills.**
**You are not your achievements.**
**You are much more than that!**

What are positive and negative outcomes of these areas of fusion?

What are some possible consequences for you if you notice these connections but take no effective action to separate who you are from what you do?

**What are the potential consequences of taking immediate effective action?**

## *Journal Entries January 2022 – December 2022*

### *8th February, 2022*

*What is going on?*

*I have just had two weeks off as sick leave. I returned to work on Monday and did some office stuff in the morning, catching up on emails and starting my CEO report for the upcoming Board meeting. In the afternoon, I joined the crew and did some painting of the dining room thanks to another COVID interruption. **I really felt stressed with painting.** I knew it was just a first coat, but my perfectionism kicked in hard, and my anxiety went through the roof. Was I doing it right? **In my mind, the drive for perfection was so high, it had become debilitating. I even heard myself explaining to one of the team, "I don't want to make a mistake." Talk about pressure.***

*This whole return to work plan is proving to be a debacle. What I can't explain is the wave of emotion, stress, anxiety that I felt this morning. My chest hurts. I am just emotional and can't breathe deep enough to get sufficient oxygen in. And once again, I am angry for feeling like this. I am wondering about my capacity to do my job. This is not good.*

*While out riding, I was thinking about what I would think of other CEOs taking the time to get out in the fresh air before work and looking after themselves. I would say, "Good on you, well done, it is important that you do that." **So why can't I give myself permission to do this? I have this constant battle about what a CEO should be doing. The truth is, I don't really know and that just adds fuel to the fire of misperception of incompetence and of wasting time.***

*I really wish I could name this feeling, so I can beat it. I have rested. I am taking my medication. I am reading. I am exercising, I should be feeling better.*

*And I should be able to get on with life and my role. This is annoying. I just need to release the pent-up frustration with my incredible lack.*

**So, what do I really think about myself at the moment?**

- *Gutless*
- *Useless*
- *Pathetic*
- *Wasting time*
- *Incompetent*
- *Fraud*
- *Imposter*
- *Fake*
- *Poser*

*Yvette told me this morning to be kind to myself… As you can see, that isn't going so well.*

**I don't want to be like this – It is embarrassing.** *Yes, I care what others think. I am glad that our current staff do not carry the old story where I had to prove myself to be working. Unfortunately, I am still carrying this.* **The powerful need to do more, be more, achieve more and be seen in the process overwhelms me, and I don't know how to move beyond it.**

**2nd March, 2022**

*One problem is that I don't really know what my best self looks like, or who I am. One realisation this morning is that I have tried to imitate Bill. The image that hooked me was that the leader is always on, always working, always ready, always dreaming, planning, etc. I have subconsciously taken this as an ideal model for the CEO to adopt. However, as is now very apparent, I cannot work without ceasing. While I might be called to the mission, there is no reward or benefit in copying Bill's mode of operation.*

### 10th March, 2022

### Great insights from my psychologist:

- *Expectation – reality = suffering score*

*He used a golf analogy, which I completely understood. I cannot hit the fairway which is 50m wide – although I expect I should be able to. I land in the trees and expect that I can split a one metre gap between two trees to make a shot towards the green. My expectations are so far from reality that my suffering continues to increase as I hit the tree and the ball bounces backwards deeper into the rough, only to try the ridiculous again and lose another shot.*

*The final trigger before this long break off work was reviewing the strategic plan. We are about two years behind, so my method is simply to add this year's KPIs to the unfulfilled expectations of the past couple of years. This simply adds expectation on expectation and moves further and further away from reality and my suffering increases even more.*

*Virgil also identified how our focus can affect our mental state:*

- *Focusing backwards leads to depression*
- *Focusing forwards leads to anxiety*
- *Staying in the present brings peace*

*I did get a call from Yvette that another former staff member, was now calling to see how I was – very frustrating. The old system is very strong and kicks into gear at the first hearing of any news, good, bad, or otherwise. Yes, everyone is very well meaning – but the long and short of it is this is Christian gossip at its finest, and this is the system I fought to remove for so many years. I do not need to be judged as I have been in the past. History has unfortunately revealed that this system and some of these people will never change. So, allowing that to create frustration for me probably won't help me move forward.*

### 16th March, 2022

*Well, my expectations and reality appear to be running in a parallel universe that is unlikely to ever meet.*

*I think the major problem is my internal, unspoken expectations of myself. These create genuine drama, stress, and tension. These internal expectations appear to increase or become problematic around events, milestones, and significant markers. **Yesterday was my 48th birthday. In my head, the lingering story of frustration and disappointment that I am currently in this physical and mental state plays on my mind. I'm not sure what I was thinking – hey it's my birthday everything is good now! Just a little deluded, but worth a crack.** Then there is the disappointment of not being further along the track in terms of recovery. Add my birthday ideal to the impending deadline of returning to work and not feeling ready and it is easy to see the ever-expanding gap between my expectations and my reality.*

### 31st March 2022

*I have felt the anxiety rising all week. Much of this is about the date of my returning to work. After some discussion about faith and the Christian journey, Virgil said that the way forward is living a disciplined, healthy life every day where you practice what you believe. Head knowledge is one thing, but if I actually believe what I say I believe, then I would do things differently.*

*Bottom line – this is my dying to self-moment. This is my Gethsemane. Even Jesus prayed to the Father to take the cup from him. But he submitted his will to the Father and obediently died on the cross. I need to let go of fear, control and pride and put self to death. Without death, there is no resurrection, no new life. I am struggling with knowing how to do this, and to be completely honest, I am really annoyed that I am still here. In my thinking, I have done everything I can and should be ready by now. You can hear the self-focus even as I type – this is the point of the whole matter. I am still trying to be the hero of my story. Rest, recuperate, get through this burnout, and come back better than ever. The problem is, I am trying to control it. I want it done my way, and in my time.*

*Father God, I need more help.*

### 7th April, 2022

*What I foolishly did not see coming in my doctor's appointment today was a doubling of my medication. Mmmm?*

***In my head, nine weeks was a long time and really should have been enough.*** *Although I had been warned about the three steps forwards, two steps back kind of journey, I did not expect the steps back to make me feel like I was right back at the beginning.* ***I am disappointed in myself. What am I doing back here? How am I still here? I thought I had made some progress. So, in typical fashion, I wallowed for a time, self-medicated with two glasses of red wine and tried hard to ignore the harassment of negative thoughts and feelings. I have fed this Beast many times.*** *It is what I have always done and look where it has landed me.*

**19*th* April 2022**

I have recently experienced quite a high level of anxiety, and I realised I was simply not ready. This led me to a meeting with the Board and another appointment with my doctor who ultimately extended my certificate through until the 6*th* June. I may not need all the time, but I certainly needed to go beyond the 19*th*, and I needed a release from the pressure of a looming deadline.

**9th May, 2022**

Well, the journey continues. The battle for my mind rages with unrelenting vigour and I drift between truth and the pit of mud that is my mind. If I remain focused on the thoughts my mind produces, it is next to impossible to move forward positively. I am disappointed at not being able to return to work. I am a failure! I am just wasting time!

**11th May, 2022**

Decision making remains a challenge and the mornings are difficult. **Just choosing what to wear is proving a regular problem.** One challenge with clothing is what it represents, and the image I wish to portray. How do I want others to perceive me? How do I want to present to others? Am I overdressed, underdressed, or am I a try hard? Or am I on the money? I suspect a fear of what others think fuels this. A fear of other's perceptions and judgements. A fear of failing. I never realised I was so image conscious. Why am I so concerned about this?

**17th May, 2022**

I have just returned from climbing the pyramid at Girraween National Park A very steep walk that takes approximately two hours to return.

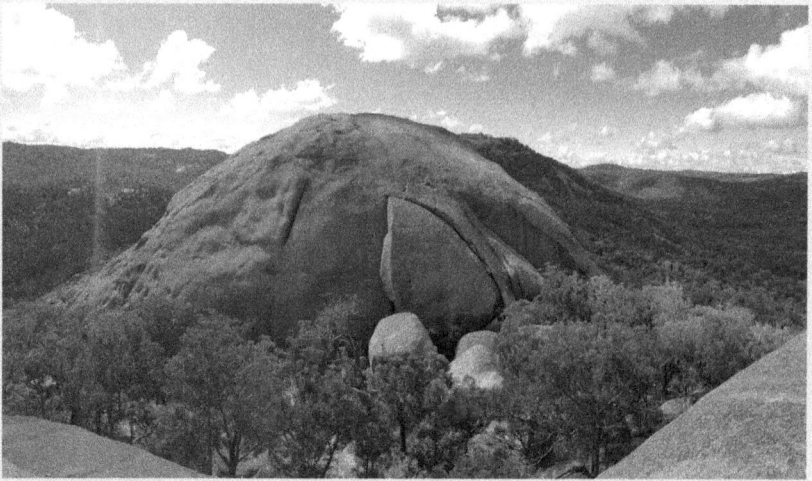

## 9. The Pyramid – Girraween National Park

*Whilst at the top of the pyramid today, I had two primary thoughts. The first is that we are explorers by nature. God gave us the earth to have dominion over, to search, to explore, to use. He provided everything we will ever need on the earth and the processes he put in place. The second thing I realised is that we don't stay at the mountaintop for long. Even when we think we are staying longer than others, we stay at the peak for a relatively short period of time compared to the effort and time that the journey took.*

***I have always been a destination man.*** *Get there as fast as you can and enjoy it and then move on. One problem with this approach is the good times, the times of peak success get shorter and shorter, and ultimately less fulfilling.* ***This journey is more frightening and of significantly greater difficulty than any hike or mountain. Being prepared to look your real self in the eye, discover your motivations, thoughts, values, beliefs, and attitudes and then confront them if necessary is hard work.***

*24th May, 2022*

*Yesterday I returned to work for the first time since mid-February.*

*I had said I was fine and happy with the go-slow approach. But truthfully, I wanted to show everyone: myself, the Executive, Chris, and everyone else that I was not only on track, but that I was back. Ready to go. Part time was just a precautionary action.* **My hidden motives were to prove to everyone that I was back. Argh…. This is the same story that got me here; Now I'm just doing that in recovery.**

*2nd June, 2022*

*Virgil asked about how the return to work went and I indicated I had worked slightly more hours than we had agreed. His recommendation was 10 hours per week, and we had agreed to three mornings in the first week and three after-noons in the second week.* **Virgil interrupted my explanation quickly and explicitly painted the picture for me: The condition is an addiction—I am a workaholic. To put it in perspective, it is like an alcoholic leaving an AA meeting and walking into the first pub and ordering a drink.** *I failed at the first challenge. The professional medical advice/contract was to do 10 hours a week. Approx three hours per day. At the very first opportunity, I fed the Beast and worked longer. Motives and intentions are not the issue here. It is the ability to control myself in any situation. The sad truth is, I am not in control. I still think I can beat this and that I have some level of control.*

*30th June, 2022*

*During the past fortnight, I have been doing really well. I have been diligently following the return-to-work plan. It has been good to simply switch off and head home. Last week I handled 3 x 5-hour days relatively well. I still needed sleep in the afternoons when I came home, but this was good, and I could accept this.* **This week has been a slightly different story. The intent was to do 4 x 5-hour days and see where I was at physically. I decided to work four days straight and as you may have guessed, I am still in a pretty low state apparently.**

*14th July, 2022*

**The battle to live in the land of reality is harder than we may think.** *Being present in the here and now is an arduous task. The longer this week has gone on, the harder I have found it to remain positive and simply be ok with the facts of each day. The battle that rages in my mind makes the simple seem really complex and difficult to understand.* **My mind begins its field day with questioning whether I will ever get back to full strength and energy. I mean seriously - I have already been resting for six months.**

*I just want to be better, and I can feel myself trying to fight everything, my thoughts, reality, everything. I end up just feeling agitated. The result has been a steady decline in thinking and my mental state.*

*4th August, 2022*

*Met with Anthony and Jack this morning to discuss RTW plan. They have had a conversation with Chris, where he asked them directly if they thought I was ready to return as CEO. Unfortunately, they answered no! Their response was primarily based on the ongoing level of fatigue, the sense of overwhelm and limited decision-making capacity I had displayed. I probably should have expected this but feels like a kick in the guts. Anthony suggested that the fatigue and sense of overwhelm with decision making are symptoms and probed some deeper questions about the root cause. He asked me to search why am I so driven to get back and be healthy. Why is being the CEO important? I have done almost nothing other than to try and answer this question and yet I am still here; right where I started! In my linear thinking, I thought I was almost out of the mud pit and have been enjoying returning to work and improving my ability. This makes me feel like I am only just getting into the mud.*

### *9th August, 2022*

*Who am I? Why is work such a driving force? Why is my value directly tied to what I do and what I can contribute? It has been hard coming back and feeling like others are doing my job better than me. **The really hard questions asked by Anthony were still ringing in my ears – what if I never came back as CEO? Am I ok if I am not the CEO?** In my head, this would suck. I have been working my butt off to achieve this. I believe I am called to this organisation and have the skills and abilities to do the job. Unfortunately, even the most simple things are causing me a lot of struggles. And to make matters worse, others are doing better than me.*

*Fatigue is insane! I have no control over fatigue, or how obviously visible this is to everyone else. I feel quite pathetic. I lack motivation for everything. No matter how hard I work, I always feel like I am failing to prove myself. My RTW plan is, once again, unrealistic. I have set myself up to fail, again. This will be three times I have failed to meet my own deadline. **I am so disappointed and frustrated with myself at the moment.***

### *14th September, 2022*

*Had a session with Virgil today and discussed the proposal put forward by Chris to consider not returning to CEO role until after LSL. He was really pleased and encouraged me to engage in the process and make the greatest psychological advantage out of this experience. It is not just in the trip that is of value, but also in the planning.*

*Again, we talked a lot about the Christian metaphors of dying to self, and the transition narratives, such as Moses to Joshua, Jesus to Christ etc… These metaphors all included a message of dying. For example, Moses the hero who led the people out of slavery did not enter Canaan. He died in the desert. Only Joshua and Caleb would transition into the future and Joshua also needed to transition from 2nd in charge to the leader. He needed to be a different person than what he was in the past. Even Jesus went through this transformation to the point where the disciples and his closest followers did not recognise him after the resurrection until he revealed himself.*

*Virgil's comments were direct: The hero who leads you into the wilderness must stay there. The Darren who led me to this point cannot enter the future. He went on to say not to panic in the wilderness; you can't know what he (the new Darren) will look like.*

*He also described that progression in a spiritual sense is not about becoming more, doing more or being more. It is about the letting go and losing yourself. It is a process where the self dissolves so that Christ can truly live in me. The goal of this part of my journey is to surrender my Self. Without my Self dying, I will not be free to progress. I will stay in the wilderness and perhaps die there. If I cannot die to my Self, my dreams, my visions, my goals then I may well die fighting this losing battle.*

*I genuinely feel like I am wandering in the wilderness without a map, isolated and confused.*

*This transition is not about Darren being the CEO…*

*It is about Darren Being.*

**26th September, 2022**

**I am really nervous about spending time with the Lord.** *First, I am not sure what to ask, or even how to approach things. Second, my faith and trust are low, not that I don't believe, but I am uncertain of how he will respond to me. Again, I am trying to control things and my Self does not want to die. I know the CEO needs to die. My Self, my flesh needs to die. I need to let go of all the dreams and visions and ways I thought things would work out.* **This journey is confusing and difficult.** *Fear is keeping me in a place of resistance, and I am looking for excuses and jobs to fill my time.*

**25th October, 2022**

*My motivation is very low at the moment. The fatigue has resurfaced, and my internal dialogue continues to be as confused as ever.* **I have spiralled down since our last Executive meeting.** *After processing I think this discussion was the trigger – and chiefly the fact that I am not in control of my future. At the upcoming Board meeting, which is tomorrow, we will discuss and approve Jack staying in the role of acting CEO until I return from LSL. This is logical and good, but it is clear evidence I am not where I want to be. This is not only my personal assessment but also the assessment of others.* **I think one challenge for me is the feeling of being completely exposed.** *Because of my brutal honesty, I have relinquished complete control of my future to others.*

*In trying to unearth some of the deeper things, Anthony challenged me to think about some rules I live by and then to challenge if they are true or valid as well as consider who made them.*

*So, what are some of my rules:*

1.  *I succeed only when I work*
2.  *At work, I succeed only when I do more, produce more and better than anyone else*
3.  *Life is about winning and losing / success and failure*
4.  *I fail when I leave work early*
5.  *I fail when I don't have the energy or capacity to fulfil my role or do the things I want to do*
6.  *God is distant, and hard to find and harder to connect with*
7.  *Being well is demonstrated by outcomes.*
    a.  *"You will be known by the fruit of your life/actions" (Matthew 7:20)*

*28th October, 2022*

*Virgil suggested my struggles reflect that there is no space between me and my thoughts and that unfortunately, I have agreed with some of the less helpful thoughts and they have become fused.*

*Regarding work he challenged me to give this story a name. The best I could come up with was:* **"My stupid work story."** *If this were a movie, it would be pretty lame:* **Work, sleep, work, work, die.** *When I take this a step further and combine this story with my concept of purpose and calling, there is very little joy in this story. The drive to keep working removes all satisfaction with any success achieved. The only satisfaction is work. Success and achievement are just expectations, not positive outcomes of this story. Work is the goal, and the means.* **This is a stupid story. However, it is one that I have lived for as long as I can remember.**

**2nd November, 2022**

Work has become an idol in my life and fear has been a major driving force for me. Fear of man. Fear of not being enough. Fear of failing etc. Confusion has been an issue because my mind has not been clear. Further, I have agreed with every story my mind has told creating cognitive fusion.

**14th November, 2022**

The line between right and wrong, or success and failure is so thin, and my mind quickly wants to challenge any result. **It is like living with every decision being reviewed by a DRS system in a game of cricket.** This confusion and constant barrage of negative thoughts, whether I am making good decisions or bad, is a reasonable indicator that I am not "well" and need to continue the journey. **I don't want to fail at getting better.**

**27th November, 2022**

Today, I woke up feeling extremely tired again. I am aware of just how fast my mind likes to draw assumptions and make conclusions. **When I look at my face in the mirror in the morning and see how dark my eyes are, my mind goes straight into negative overdrive and suggests that today will be a difficult day, and that I am worse than I thought I should be. I am still fighting these thoughts, trying to swim upstream if you like. This accelerates the fatigue and multiplies the negative thoughts, feelings, and emotions. I know I am feeding the "Beast".** Yet strangely, I seem quite content to work myself until my body battery has completely bottomed out, almost like a badge of honour. This is the model of my family, so it is not surprising that this is deeply engraved into my psyche. I do not agree with it, or like the outcome, but changing my actions and beliefs is difficult.

## 2nd December, 2022

Christmas party this afternoon! There is a great vibe on site this morning. People in Christmas gear, lots of laughing and fun around the site, even so, all the work is being done. Everywhere I looked, I saw people doing their jobs, engaging with young people, cleaning, preparing, following up. You name it; the work was being done. Apart from the Christmas clothing, it could be day one of the year. This is a fantastic example of the culture. People have simply given their 100% for every group, every day of every program, and all the other days in between. What a privilege to be part of the crew. **For me, the revelation of a couple of weeks ago simply gets a little louder. I am not required – everything continues on and thrives without me.**

## 28th December, 2022

What still surprises me is just how quick the fatigue returns after any physical activity. The battle in my head is instantly on. I am not trying to prove anything. I am deliberately resting, but then the thoughts and questions about readiness come in. If I can't handle a couple of hours on the computer focusing on the trip of a lifetime and then play some mini golf with the kids, then? I am determined to not let this thought process get out of hand, but I am just acknowledging the anxiety that rises and the fatigue that sets in. I seem to have this inbuilt filter that says I am all good now; I have rested for a few days, yada, yada, yada. This is one of the great deceptions that I need to monitor. As I have expressed many times, I have a deep internal expectation that is motivated by what I think I should be doing. I should be good to go by now. I should be fine. The inner story and belief say that I have rested enough, now get on with it. Get back to work. It is quite a mocking belief… that yells loudly in my head: "Seriously, how much rest do you need?"

# PART 3

THE DAWN OF REALITY

# CHAPTER 7

# FACING REALITY

## NOVEMBER 2022.

I am cooked. I have now tried and failed multiple times to return to work. In my communication with others, I had given up on returning to my role as CEO. Jack was doing a fantastic job, and I was simply not up to it. I could not work for any extended period and my capacity was severely limited. Decision making was beyond me, and apart from some minor interpersonal interactions, my effectiveness and productivity were zero. The Executive could see this clearly and made it possible for me to just do whatever I needed through until the end of the year. To ease my anxiety associated with a decreasing bank of sick leave hours, the company graciously allowed me to come and go as I was able with one clear focus - **"Just get better"**. This was now the only conversation. My focus shifted slightly for the first time in two and a half years. I just needed to get better. This was not about being the CEO anymore. It was time for Darren to be Darren. The CEO's position in the driver's seat was uncomfortable and his grip on my identity had just shifted, just slipped a little. Could it be that I, Darren, was actually the real deal? Could it be that I was not the CEO?

As you may have guessed, the CEO would not let go without a fight. Still deeply entrenched in my inner belief structure, the CEO had strong hopes of returning. Ok, he had accepted the proposal not to return to the role until after long service leave, but all going well he should be fully recovered by then - refreshed, recharged, renewed, and ready for the next chapter.

## BRUTAL HONESTY

One attribute that has always worked for me, but also sometimes against me, is my brutal honesty. In my efforts to lead by example with transparency and vulnerability, I have never withheld my honest assessment of situations and how I have contributed to them. Unfortunately, in this situation, this honesty would not serve me well. On my return to work in January 2023, I wrote the following summary for the Executive and the Board:

### *Darren Update January 4th 2023*

- ***I am generally going ok,*** *although am keenly aware of how quick the body battery can be depleted*
- ***I am very conscious of my mental state,*** *and at times this can increase the level of anxiety*
  - *For example, I could sense anxiety rising in the lead up to returning and all the unanswered "what if" questions*
- ***I have had mostly good days over the break,*** *which is good as I have virtually done nothing but rest*
  - *It would be a real concern if I was down for long given the break*
- *My subconscious and sometimes conscious mode of handling situations is to go big… to give everything I have got*
  - *For example, at the Christmas party I could feel myself dropping and starting to just watch proceedings from a distance*

- ○ *I even said to Yvette I had better keep moving or I will drop*
- ○ *So, I danced a lot and enjoyed the wine and kept going until the very end, and then I dropped the next day*
- ○ *This is probably not a sustainable method of handling functions and engagements*
- *I still get caught by surprise when I bottom out. This has occurred numerous times including:*
  - ○ *Shopping – no real surprise*
  - ○ *Time on the computer – sustained concentration*
  - ○ *Working on things that matter – where I have a level of responsibility (banks, phones etc…)*
  - ○ *Technology – setting up tablet*
  - ○ *Large crowds*
  - ○ *Physical activity – when my body battery is already lowish*
- *Things that give me energy*
  - ○ *Reading*
  - ○ *Painting*
  - ○ *Physical activity – at a fairly low level*
    - ■ *Riding my bike*
    - ■ *Walking*
    - ■ *Surfing*
  - ○ *Time with Yvette*
  - ○ *Just resting*
- *Concerns with work on return*
  - ○ *Loads of "what if" and unresolved questions*
    - ■ *What if I can't handle things?*
    - ■ *What if I don't return at the end of LSL?*
    - ■ *What if I'm not able to work in the first half of 2023?*
    - ■ *If I were not to return, what would I do?*

- *What if I can't get back to work at the level I have been?*
- *Am I useful?*
- *What will I be doing?*
- *What will my role be?*

- *Managing expectations – particularly mine is important*
  - *My mind says I have rested enough, now get on with it (this is the "Beast" talking)*
- *Actions required:*
  - *I will need to observe how I go in the first couple of weeks and then arrange an appointment with the doctor for an updated certificate*
  - *I have not currently got any more sessions booked in with the Psychologist – this may be required*
  - *Clarifying roles and expectations for first term through until LSL*

## CAN YOU BELIEVE THE LEVEL OF STUPIDITY I JUST DISPLAYED?

Who would read this and not be incredibly concerned? To make matters worse – I had spent a couple of hours putting it together. Seriously! The outcome would be a very cautious continuation of the return-to-work program and an ever-increasing sense of anxiety. I had experienced the depths of depression early in the journey, but until now, had never really been overly anxious about anything. However, as you can see from the list of "what if" questions in the summary, there was a lot to be apprehensive about.

One of the primary concerns was in relation to my depleting bank of sick leave hours. You need to understand my history here. Until this time, I just didn't take sick leave, I was living from my core belief to show no pain. Sickness in my opinion was weakness and mental sickness was not even valid. It was not a reason not to work, just something to work through. From 2014 through 2020, I had used a total of 57 hours of sick leave. That is less than a day per year. Included in those 57 hours were several days where I stayed home to look after my wife and kids, but I was not actually sick. From the time this journey began, through until long service leave in April 2023, I had used over 1300 hours of sick leave. Praise God I had such a bank of leave to draw from, but I was now significantly concerned about what my capacity might be on return from long service leave. How would I manage if I had not completely recovered? What if I needed to continue working reduced hours, but had no sick leave left? If I could not return full time, would I have to take a pay cut? The burning anxiety in my chest was unrelenting and painful. I would often try to rub my sternum or have a cool drink to soothe it. Nothing worked!

The other thing that was now painfully obvious was that I was no longer employed as the CEO. Jack was no longer the Acting CEO. The Board had officially appointed him as the new CEO. For the time being, they assigned me the role of Executive Director, and although the role suited the situation, I faced significant challenges in addressing the longevity of my tenure and continuation upon my return. The CEO did not like losing his title. But at the hands of others, the battle had shifted and the CEO, for the first time, was caught off guard.

**Facing reality was now unavoidable and I was out of options. Let me provide a summary:**

- My identity was so entangled with the role of CEO that Darren had essentially ceased to exist
- I was suffering complete Burnout – Physical, Mental, Emotional, Spiritual and Social
- I was a middle-aged man with significantly reduced physical capacity
  - It now appears that this physical capacity is unlikely to ever increase again

- Any level of decision-making was overwhelming and well beyond me
- I had no capacity to handle any level of responsibility
- I was questioning my core beliefs and my faith
- Many of my inner stories and tightly held beliefs were exposed as false, inaccurate, incomplete or insufficient
- The well-developed and comprehensive skill set that had provided me with success until this point was inadequate to overcome this current challenge or to navigate the journey ahead
- I actively avoided social engagements and reduced the size of my world to protect myself
- I felt judged as a failure by the founding director and others for losing the heart of the company
- The doctor diagnosed me with a major depressive disorder, and I still require daily medication
- The psychologist had determined that I was a workaholic – an addict with a messiah complex
- I had set up and engaged in multiple return to work programs and failed them all – never getting beyond 25 hours per week with any consistency, and very little productivity
- I had used more than 1300 hours of personal leave between the end of 2021 and 2023 to aid recovery, and all efforts had failed to see me effectively return to work
- I did not know if I would return to full-time work after long service leave
- My future income and livelihood were now on the line
- I was no longer the CEO. The Board removed this and re-titled me as an Executive Director
  - However, there remained a distinct lack of clarity about what I should be doing

- I had lost the confidence of the Executive and the Board. They were seeking professional advice regarding options and how to proceed
- The company was thriving without me
  - I was clearly not required
- My family, especially my wife, became exhausted from carrying the load and covering for my deficiencies. The strain on them was clearly visible

Facing reality was not limited to the start of 2023. This was the last peak, so to speak and as you can see, reality was hitting like a sledgehammer. You see, there is a significant gap between knowing something to be true and accepting it. Identifying reality and continuing to fight with or against it is exhausting and ultimately brings death and this was the reality I was facing. I was down. And I was not sure if I would be getting up again. This battle was rapidly reaching its climax and decision time was rapidly approaching. The decision was the battle. There was no part of my life or my future path that reflected any level of certainty and absolutely everything was on the line. Who am I? What do I really believe? Am I the CEO, or am I Darren?

The CEO was exceptionally close to victory but had exhausted almost every reserve of energy left in the tank. The CEO and I had been trading body blows for some time now and the CEO's defence system of success, achievement, and more work was crumbling and his grip on my identity was slipping. With his offsider the Beast, the CEO had been controlling things for such a long time, there was simply no way this was going to be easy.

Darren's hand was being forced. He could no longer agree with the CEO, there was too much at stake. Failure in this battle would not only kill Darren, but it could significantly damage Yvette and the family. Their livelihoods were now on the line. Darren had no choice but to stand and face reality. **Darren had to kill the CEO!**

# REFLECTION

## Leadership Lessons

- Get someone to check every piece of work before submitting or presenting
  - This is important in every area, but especially critical in personal situations
- Honesty, transparency and vulnerability are extremely important and demonstrate authenticity and integrity
  - However, consider your language. For example, in my summary the first phrase read:
    - "I am generally going ok" - This raises immediate red flags
  - A constructive reframe could be:
    - "I am continuing to improve and am focusing on increasing my physical and mental capacity" - This is positive and highlights actions that are helping me move forward
- Title's matter to people – Even you
  - If you change a title, make sure you explain the context and provide clarity for the new role
  - I would highly recommend not making this decision without significant discussion, consultation, and collaboration with the person whose title is being changed
  - Check the legality of the action; a title change may be considered a demotion, thus leaving you vulnerable to HR challenges, increased stress, and discontent among valued staff.

Where are you at? Can you summarise your story so far?

How old are you? Are you still expecting to work and play like you did in your mid 20s? Do you need more time to recover from work or exercise or both?

Can you identify your strengths, weaknesses, core beliefs and stories?

Is there a level of separation between you and your role?

What can you do to create distance between your role and identity?

Facing and embracing reality is hard. But living in denial is harder. I have spent most of this journey fighting against reality and I have suffered for it. Please take a moment to face your own realities.

# CHAPTER 8

# FINDING GOD

From November 2022 and into 2023, I had no option but to face reality. I then had to make some decisions about the future. Digging deeper than ever before into my core beliefs and the stories I had believed for so long was incredibly painful. What was real? What was fake? Who was I? Who was Darren? Where is he? Where has he been? And what did he believe? Could it be that I was Darren and not the CEO?

The CEO had complete control of my identity and had worked ridiculously hard to reinforce that his ways were best. The CEO knew what was required in all situations. The CEO could handle all things. The CEO did not want to acknowledge God at all. Despite working in his service, the CEO truly believed that he was responsible for success, achievement, and provision. The CEO had become a representation of my sinful nature, and it was now becoming abundantly clear that if I, Darren, did not kill the CEO, I would live the rest of my life believing that God didn't care, couldn't or wouldn't heal and won't provide.

So somewhat courageously, I finally addressed my relationship with God and began to challenge some of my core beliefs about him. Is God good? Does he care? Why is he so distant and difficult to connect with? Where is the power of the Holy Spirit in my life? After all these years of faithful service, joyful tithing, actively giving and supporting others, living a life of committed dedication and passionate leadership, why am I not further down the track? My extreme disappointment with God was front of mind, as was my frustration with our financial position and his perceived lack of provision, guidance, wisdom, and healing.

Have you ever noticed that faith really matters in the areas of life that matter most to you? It is one thing to have aspirational ideals and things you say you believe but, push really does come to shove when your faith genuinely affects your lifestyle. This is where the rubber meets the road. When the practical outworking of your faith directly influences your actions and your capacity to do what you want to do.

Interestingly, Virgil asked me about my salvation story during this time period. How did I come to Christ and what has been the result? I shared how at four years of age I was so moved by a guest speaker's sermon at Sunnybank Baptist about how Jesus died on the cross for us, I had to leave the building. I remember sitting in the car, a red XY Falcon station wagon, with my mother. I was bawling my eyes out and my mum was really concerned. She gently asked me what the problem was, and I told her that, *"I would die for Jesus."* Her wise response was simple and profound. *"That is great, Darren, but will you live for him?"* The answer was a resounding yes, and I have lived a deliberate life of service to Jesus ever since. When I was 16 years old, I was baptized in water, and I prayed for the infilling of the Holy Spirit around the same time.

But there were a couple of fundamental problems with my thinking etched into my core from the very start. It was not until this session with Virgil that I saw my error in perception and subsequent belief. First, the preaching of the day when I was first saved was hellfire and brimstone. "Repent. Be prepared. Jesus could return very soon, possibly even tonight, and if you're not saved, you'll face eternal damnation in hell." It was a fear-based message and my image of God from this very early age was of a judgmental God. You know the kind - thunderbolts and lightning, very, very frightening!

The second misconception and subsequent belief was that my salvation depended on what I could do for God. And I was happy to do whatever I could. My whole life would be about fulfilling his calling on my life and serving him. I loved God and was so grateful for what Jesus did for me, I simply wanted to do what I could in return. I did not understand that this salvation was a free gift. Although I understood it theoretically, I didn't actually live it as a reality. And right from the very point of salvation, my focus was on works which were motivated by fear. This deep internal belief had been strengthening the CEO's operating system for years and had become a pillar of the CEO's identity. What could be more noble than to work harder than anyone else in the service of God Almighty? Is it any wonder I, Darren, had struggled to develop a close personal relationship with Jesus?

With the CEO in control of my identity, my relationship with God was not only distant and shallow, but deeply damaged. With the CEO's win/loss framework, there was no room for failure, and no room for things to work out differently to what the CEO expected. This led to playing the comparison game and deep spiritual disappointment.

## THE COMPARISON GAME

How is your comparison game? Mine, to be honest, is never far from my mind. For example, at the time of writing, we had been out of the property market for many years and were working hard to raise sufficient funds to get back in. Having our own home again would be a dream come true and would provide a level of financial security after so many years of paying off someone else's mortgage. Many of my friends have made their way into the market and their decisions have moved them forward. Some have multiple properties and continue to build equity and appear to go from strength to strength. I have seen many young families, even people I have employed, make their way into the market. In one sense, nothing could make me a prouder boss than providing the opportunity and capacity for someone to move forward in this way. For the CEO, this was like a badge of honour, a genuine success. But for me, Darren, this comparison game often ended in despair and could trigger a major depressive spiral.

Please hear me, I am exceptionally grateful for the life we have lived. Along the way, my wife and I made the choice to prioritise lifestyle over equity, and we have been blessed. We decided to provide our four kids with a private education, and they have never gone without. Throughout our adventures, we have travelled around the country in a caravan, relished annual beach vacations, and had the opportunity to explore different countries on several occasions. We made our choices, and we are settled with them, mostly. But it doesn't stop you looking sideways and comparing yourself to others. By the way, if you are not yet aware, **it is impossible to win the comparison game.** It doesn't matter what you compare, it is a losing game. And worse still, when you play and lose there is a reinforced, ever-present, ever-deepening sense of failure.

Unfortunately, the CEO loved to play this game, and he was good at it, or at least he thought so. The CEO mistakenly believed that he could not lose. You see, the CEO never viewed loss negatively, which is incredibly healthy. This is called failing forward, and is a very powerful framework for gaining perspective, learning, adapting, and growing. However, the problem was that the CEO took this to the extreme and falling short of expectations or failing only ever served as fuel for more determination and hard work. It didn't matter to the CEO what resources were in the bank, physical, mental, or otherwise. The comparison game always ended with the CEO, in cahoots with the Beast, working harder and longer. And for me, Darren, that ultimately resulted in failure and burnout.

One example of an uncomfortable comparison occurred in the back end of 2022. Jack was doing a better job as Acting CEO than I had been doing as the "real CEO". He seemed to have an extraordinary capacity reservoir and loved the opportunity to say yes to things, worrying later about how to make it happen. And he would consistently deliver. Jack and Anthony, the remaining Executive, had not faulted in my absence. They had absolutely thrived. They did things differently, but they were excelling. The company was flourishing. The staff were going from strength to strength. Morale was at an all-time high. Excitement, commitment, and engagement were off the charts, and I became exceedingly conscious that I was not required. Ouch! When I discussed this with Virgil he understood and was relatively unphased. Typical! Using another practical application, he told me to go home and put my hand in a bucket of water and notice what happens when I took it out. I did this, and the results couldn't have been more confronting or deeply depressing. As I took my hand out, the water simply filled every space with barely a ripple. In fact, the level of the water would barely register any decline at all. Truth bomb – I am replaceable. I am not that good. I am not that important. The CEO did not like this comparison or realisation at all and made sure I, Darren, felt the full weight of this failure. Being the best or real CEO was his territory and Darren had failed.

## DISAPPOINTMENT – EVEN GOD FAILED TO COMPARE WITH MY EXPECTATIONS

Playing the comparison game even included and affected my spiritual life. The core inner beliefs and values I had held and lived by since I was a child were, for the first time, facing a reality check. I simply could not reconcile what I said I believed and my lived experience. Nothing was matching up.

I said and truly thought I was living out of the belief that God was good. That he cared. That he healed. That he provided. That he wanted a relationship with me and had a purpose for me and that he had called me into his service. For years I had been standing on scripture verses such as John 10:10 *"I come to give life and life to the full"*; Luke 6:38 *"Give and it will be given back to you, pressed down, shaken together and running over"* and Jeremiah 29:11*"I know the plans I have for you, plans to prosper you and not to harm you. Plans to give you a hope and a future."* I believed these verses with all my heart, but they were not proving to be true of my current reality. Despite many times of desperate prayer, God felt distant. I had prayed for healing and seen no results. Whenever I asked specific questions, the only thing I could hear was stony silence. Nothing! So much for a relational, caring God!

My life was unraveling at a rate of knots and everything I thought I knew was being exposed as a lie, a false reality. I was suffering deeply, my family was suffering, and we were not reaping the rewards of our faith. There was no joy, no abundance, no exciting life. Nothing made sense and I questioned everything I believed.

## CONFUSION, INCONSISTENCY, AND DISAPPOINTMENT

Let me give you a couple of examples of how I had let comparison and disappointment frame my perception of reality. When I was 13 years old, I experienced a miraculous healing of my back. Doctors diagnosed me with Scheuermann's disease, a condition where the vertebrae in your back disintegrate and cause immense pain. This gets worse over time and there is no cure. Sitting in the car on the way to school was excruciating and the doctor told me I would never play contact sport again. A fortnight after having x-rays to confirm the diagnosis, I went to church as normal with the family. A visiting speaker with a healing ministry called me out for prayer. She laid hands on my head and back and prayed for me and I felt instantly better. I was miraculously healed. There was no pain at all from that day on. I went back to the doctor later that week and he could not believe it. He sent me back for another set of x-rays and to his absolute astonishment he said, *"This is not right. Your condition should show further degeneration, but when I look at them, there appears to be genuine improvement. I don't really believe in God and all that stuff, but I have no other way to explain this. It must be a miracle."* This healing was a foundation for me. An anchor point of trust in God that I believed and no one could argue with or tell me otherwise. Incidentally, I would play many contact sports for over 20 years and never have that trouble with my back again. I would do some other injuries doing weights, but the Scheuermann's disease would never affect me again.

This experience was a foundational cornerstone of my faith. I would share it many times with my family and with others to encourage them that God is a healing God. It was our habit and custom to pray for healing, solution, provision, guidance and wisdom and He would always deliver… well, almost always. And this is where the problem was. I felt the results were inconsistent. Sometimes healing happened, sometimes it didn't.

One of the hardest and perhaps most damaging examples was in relation to my eldest son. He is a very good AFL player and was on the cusp of being drafted. At two key points in his development journey, he suffered serious injuries that would take him out of contention and rob him of any further opportunity. The first was a hip-pointer injury that stopped him from running for 11 weeks. This occurred while he was training with the Queensland under 16 team and meant that he could not take any further part in the national competition. We prayed, we believed. He even went up for prayer at church. Nothing. No healing, just disappointment, disillusionment, and lost opportunity. The second injury was truly cruel and heartbreaking. As a 19-year-old, he was asked to play for the Brisbane

Lions reserves side on a consistent basis. This was a one-year non-contracted opportunity, and the club would only select the best of the academy players. The club and coaches saw his potential and asked him if he would consider moving to Brisbane to give himself the very best chance of making it. Their words to him were very clear and encouraging, *"We want to get you on a list."* He would play several games as the only non-AFL-listed player on the reserves side, and he was feeling comfortable at that level. Only a few weeks after moving to Brisbane, an opponent tackled him, and he suffered a season-ending syndesmosis injury. Opportunity lost again. Surgery, rehabilitation, everything followed to the letter, but opportunity lost. We prayed and sought the Lord. We believed for healing, and again he went forward for prayer. Nothing. No healing. Just more disappointment, disillusionment, and lost opportunity. As Darren and Dad, I felt this deeply. I knew he trusted me and my experience, and he was ready to trust God for his own healing, but both of us were left disappointed, and to be honest, I felt it deeply. This was not fair and just did not make sense. Why would God heal me and not my son? Damage done!

The spiritual inconsistencies included my perceived shallow and somewhat distant relationship with God, and limited presence of the Holy Spirit and his power in my life. Fundamental to the Christian faith is the fact that Jesus died on the cross and rose again after three days and later ascended into heaven leaving us with the promise of the Holy Spirit as our helper until he returns at the end of the age. The book of Acts details the account of how the Holy Spirit came upon the original disciples who were praying about 50 days after Jesus had returned to his Father in heaven. The words of Jesus in Acts 1:8 are very clear regarding the influence of the Holy Spirit… *"you will receive power when the Holy Spirit comes upon you."* And later in chapter 2, we see the Holy Spirit poured out on all the gathered believers. As the Spirit filled people, they would speak in tongues, prophecy, and use the gifts given to them. In verses 38–39, Peter clearly stated that this gift of the Holy Spirit was not just for the disciples, but for all believers, both at the time and in the future. *"Repent and be baptized, every one of you, in the name of Jesus Christ for the forgiveness of your sins. And you will receive the gift of the Holy Spirit. The promise is for you and your children and for all who are far off, for all whom the Lord our God will call."*

## SHARED DISAPPOINTMENT

I had a problem - I was disappointed with God and so was the CEO. The CEO and Darren both liked things to follow a predetermined formula. In simple terms, if you do this, you get that, pretty simple really. Not unlike Newton's 1st law which states that "for every action, there is an equal and opposite reaction." From the CEO's perspective, if you work hard – you will succeed, if you don't you will fail. For Darren, if you pray and ask God for something, that is what should happen. If it does not happen this way, then God must not be true to his word, or may not be real at all.

The first seeds of doubt and disappointment were planted when I prayed for the baptism of the Holy Spirit in my teenage years. I desperately wanted to receive the gift of the Holy Spirit, and to speak in tongues like others were and experience the power of the Spirit. But it would be twelve long years of earnestly seeking the Lord for this, and even then, I would receive just one word. Just one word! Deep down, I knew I had the Spirit in me, and I knew if this was the only word I would ever receive, it would be more than enough. But I am just being brutally honest. I wanted more, and I felt disappointed. I had witnessed the Holy Spirit work powerfully on and in and through others, but in recent times I had not experienced this myself. Even as I type this, I know it is not true but what I am trying to show you is that I had been shaken to the core, and I was deeply disappointed. You cannot live the blessed life I have without the hand of God and the indwelt presence of His Holy Spirit. However, I felt there needed to be more, and all the things God said he would do, well – why on earth don't they happen to me or my family?

The comparison game can be quite brutal in the professional world. For example, a long-time friend and mentor of mine, Michael, is the CEO of a school that now has six campuses. He is incredibly inspirational and relational and one of the most gifted storytellers, vision-casters, and leaders you will ever meet. Not only that he builds others up, but he also trains, inspires, and gives opportunity for people to excel. We have worked closely over the years, and he genuinely invests in me as a person and friend. But I must admit that when I play the comparison game with Michael and those he has trained, it does not take long before I feel inadequate and somewhat intimidated. And don't get me started on Jack and Anthony. They have done my job better than I have.

## FINDING GOD THROUGH REFLECTION AND PRAYER

My wife has been truly exceptional throughout this entire journey and has helped me process my thoughts. From the start I realised my thoughts were not always accurate and I invited her to be honest with me. We would sit on the couch most afternoons and she would read my daily reflection out loud. On many occasions, she was upset and saddened at just how low I was and the depths of pain I was experiencing. And at other times, she would push back and correct my obviously flawed perceptions. After reading through my reflections in early 2023 that I was not bothered about getting back to work, Yvette helped me see that the distinct shift in motivation towards work might be a positive sign that I was finally beginning to accept reality.

The relentless battle of comparison and my internal processing would thankfully lead me to press into God and seek his revelation. For all my questioning of God and whether he cares, the truth is, sometimes God allows the situations and circumstances of life to lead us to a place of courageous honesty. It is only when all our stories and beliefs have been tested in the fire of life that we can discover the truth of who he is and what he is like. I realised that the CEO was a false identity and that my true identity was to be found in relationship with God. I had to kill the CEO and choose to trust him to be sovereign and direct my steps, then perhaps he would lead me into a different future, dare I say a better one than I had imagined. It did not matter that I could not see the future, understand the past or fully explain the present. The only truth that mattered was that he was God, and he was in control. He was kind, and he was on my side.

My courageous and honest reflection had opened my eyes to a new reality, and I felt great. I had a new sense of energy and for the first time in two and a half years, I began to accept where I was. My attitude towards the future eased. The challenging thoughts were there, but they were subdued. I began to ponder the outcome of killing the false identity that was the CEO. Perhaps, if I surrender this false identity with all his dreams and goals, passion and skills, capacity, and thoughts to God, perhaps there is hope after all?

The energy and new thinking I experienced in the first half of March 2023 were truly astounding. I almost felt like I was back. As I pressed in towards God, He spoke to me like never before. Actually, he was probably always speaking; it was just now I was paying attention, and His revelations were amazing. Loving, gentle, powerful. Ah, sweet relief - who would have thought that genuinely seeking the God of the universe might provide some answers and healing for my tormented soul?

Wow, happy days! You might expect that things would progress quickly from this point. Seek God, receive his revelation, ask him direct questions, and wait on his answer. All true and wise, and to a large degree, this is what I did. However, in keeping with my habit of total honesty, I have a confession to make. My habit is to only seek help when there are no other options. It took two and a half years of depression, anxiety, and burnout before I began to honestly seek the Lord and accept that he might know better than me. So, it probably wouldn't surprise you to know that after just a few short weeks of feeling good, my level of reflection declined, and I took control again. I was still intent on seeking the Lord, accepting things as they were and not stressing over the outcomes. However, as previously stated, events affecting our livelihoods genuinely test our faith, and a significant impact on my livelihood was imminent.

I had to address the pending suffering associated with losing control of my career and my identity. To truly follow Jesus' example of doing the Father's will would require killing the false identity of the CEO through complete surrender. And then I would also have to address the issue of what actions I would take upon my return from long service leave in early July.

Not ready to die just yet, the CEO re-entered the battle and began putting parameters around this surrender and the future. Sure Darren, you might have found God, but I am still in control…

## REFLECTION

### Leadership Lessons

- How you view God will influence everything you do as a leader
- The comparison game is a losing game – you cannot win, ever
- You are not that important – you are replaceable

What do you believe about God? Are your actions in alignment with what you say you believe? Have your experiences lined up with what you say you believe?

What is your image of God? Kind and gentle, or harsh and judgmental? Is this true?

What inner stories are you believing? Are they all true? Are these stories accurate, adequate, or sufficient for the next chapter?

Finding God may not be as daunting as you may think. I challenge you to ask him some direct questions and wait on him for his answer. My experience is that he is a lot kinder than I expected. He is generous and gracious and will only respond to your invitation… "Behold I stand at the door and knock." (Revelation 3:20)

Are you, or have you been disappointed with God?

Don't be afraid of venting and being totally honest with the Lord. Tell him what you are afraid of, tell him what you are disappointed with and share with him the stuff that you just don't understand. He is a big God. He can handle it. You might need to repent later. But he even has mercy for that.

He is after your heart, and sometimes our hearts are full of all kinds of rubbish. So, in my experience, it's better to empty the bin than just squash the lid back on and hope that nobody notices the smell.

Where have you played the comparison game? How is this working out for you?

What are the anchor points of your faith?

When and how have these been challenged?

What would you like to ask the King of the Universe today?

Will you wait and listen for his response?

## *Journal Entries January 2023 – March 2023*

### *6th January, 2023*

*I feel really foolish and now have to face the demons of capacity, desire to work and what is actually best for me in the healing process. All the concerning questions that I have raised and written now need to be answered, and I simply don't have the answers. Last night I felt really low, and today I also feel the same. Once again, I have woken with stress in the chest (tightness). I haven't felt that one for a while, but it is not unfamiliar.*

*I do not want to follow my parent's model of work until I die or continue following the model that says work is the only way you get value. I want to be well. I love to work and have been trying to increase my capacity to return to doing what I love. But once again, the contest between my flesh and my spirit rages. I* get tired and then have to deal with my rubbish. This is the model that got me here and the Beast always wants to be fed.

*I do not know what to do.*

### 17th January, 2023

*When I am tired like this, it is quite hard for me to be satisfied with what I do in a day. **Knowing that at times, I am just trying to do enough to allow me to justify making a good choice and leaving early.** The battle is to see it as a good choice, not a failure or another setback, or another example of not being enough yet. It is frustrating for me that the most productive thing I have done in a day is writing this reflection. Even this statement is not true, but this is the battle that rages.*

### 19th January, 2023

*The battle in my head in the morning is exceptionally strong, and it takes quite some time to get on top of it. I have been speaking scripture and trusting in God to deliver on his promises for me. **The battle is to choose differently – not just agree with the junk my mind throws up.***

***The challenge is real.** I know all parties are tremendously supportive, but I still feel the need to justify my position. So, I will need to choose to trust that they have my back and are happy to support my journey and direct me with advice from the professionals.*

### 23rd January, 2023

*There is nothing currently more deflating or concerning than waking up knowing I'm not recharged and already desperate to get back to sleep. On top of that, today we had to put our beautiful puppy dog, Tilly, down. She is just the best dog anyone could have and is such a part of our family.*

*A couple of great opportunities have presented themselves over the past week, and my job is to review and create a business plan for them. Needless to say, I am feeling a little overwhelmed and honestly doubt my ability to bring these opportunities to pass.*

### 1st February, 2023

*I have had about enough of going around the same bloody merry-go-round of dumb thoughts and painfully wasting time on stupid stuff. In the last four weeks we have moved our son Jack to Sydney, put Tilly down and gone to a wedding in Victoria. On top of that, I have changed medication and had to concede going to three days a week for first term. The doctor does not think I will return to the role of CEO. I have worked hard to let this go, but it still leaves me in a precarious position of what the hell am I going to do when I get back? The Board has asked for formal written reports from the doctor and the psychologist, which I completely understand and would do the same in their position. It is just a brutal reality check that things are not working for me. I really want to be well for long service leave, but at this rate that might be a pipe dream. I am trying to put this morning's feelings down to the impact of changing medication – but for goodness sake I am over this circus.*

### 9th February, 2023

*My desire to work and be productive is at the centre of everything I do and how I think. **Whatever you do Darren, don't waste time.** Is resting a waste of time? Is it ok to do nothing with a day? What is genuine rest? How do you do it? I don't particularly like watching TV all day. Social media bores me after a* short time. *Painting is good and can take several hours, but I don't always feel like it. Riding my bike is good but can take a fair amount of energy. This is something I am constantly wary of. Reading and praying is helpful, although my prayers are often shallow, and I stop short of asking the tough questions. I quickly get to the shopping list and often feel defeated, or at a loss. I don't even know what to ask for or pray about.*

*Yvette commented last night that a lot of my narrative is negative and focused on what is not, or what I have lost, or don't have at the moment. So, I really need to change this story.*

### 13th February 2023

*Thinking deeper, I am ashamed that I have burned out. I am ashamed that I am still here – in this state of mind. And I am ashamed that I have not been able to get through this. I am ashamed that I have not yet learned the lessons God has in store for me. How thick, slow, and dumb am I? I am embarrassed and disappointed, not to mention frustrated and disillusioned and really irritated. I have very little motivation and yet I am more and more concerned with the outcome of the message I am sending others.*

*Once again, I left work today feeling like a failure. I have done what I was told, because I was told, not because my attitude says this is a good thing. Or that this is any way good for me. In my head, this is just proof that I have failed again. Seriously, it has now reached the point where someone else tells me what I can and cannot do. If I continue with this attitude and behaviour, there is no use at all in even returning in compliance with the restricted times, because it won't do any good. If I cannot change my mind about what is good, right, fair, successful, in line with God, then I am screwed. Why is this so hard? Everyone else seems to make the choice and move on. What is it about me that is so stubborn and* stupid? You can tell that I am really quite frustrated. But I suppose it is better to say it here than in the board meeting.

### 14th February 2023

Obviously, I am not thinking clearly, and my mind likes to run the show. It does its job and throws up all sorts of thoughts. Unfortunately, a lot of what goes through my mind is destructive, deflating, and demoralising. And when I cannot counteract these thoughts or get them in line or simply let them go, I end up in a very low place.

Despite all my whining, and complaining, I do believe in God and that he is in control of all things, so I am consciously choosing today to follow my wife's advice and write out some scriptures to stand on. I use these currently, but I have to admit, my actions show I don't always believe what they say, or what they reflect about God's character. This is where some of my struggles are. **Apparently, I do not know better than God; who would have thought???**

### 15th February, 2023

Last night was quite an ordinary night's sleep. Every time I woke up, which unfortunately was a few, the stress was central in my chest. **The stress appeared to be related to work, and the upcoming board meeting and my current lack of capacity to just handle myself and my situation.**

Regarding the feelings in my chest, I struggle to let them be. They irritate and frustrate me and cause so much grief. To be honest, I don't like just accepting them as thoughts—especially if they are not true. The wisdom of the ACT approach is to recognise and name the emotions, thoughts and feelings and let them come and go. This is difficult and I think my struggle results from me not *"accepting" the strategy. If I'm honest, my mind says, "That doesn't work - this is just some sort of psychobabble garbage."*

### 20th February 2023

*I really struggled to sleep last night, with an ever-present struggle with my thoughts ranging from insecurity to lack of capacity to anxiety about the future. The ball of stress sat firmly in my chest all day yesterday and the fatigue was immense. All I wanted to do was go to sleep to get some respite from thinking about things.*

***There is currently very little at work that is bringing me joy or satisfaction.*** *I drive in slow and feel pain in my chest. Largely unproductive, I leave once again disappointed and discouraged. I just don't feel like doing anything. **I am sick of this merry-go-round of useless thoughts and actions.***

### 23rd February 2023

*Wow, an interesting week. Just when you think things are moving forward, the struggle kicks in even harder. I have spent some time with the Lord at Ravensbourne. To be honest, this time was more of a rant than anything. An explosion of frustration that has been building for a while. 'Lord, I repent of my approach and the words I used and the lack of reverence and awe for who you are. My arrogance and self-righteousness led the way again. Please forgive me. My concept of you, and therefore my reluctance to ask questions, is based in fear. **My perception is probably based on my picture of you as a judgemental God waiting to punish or discipline me for my error and lack. I'm also fearful of what you might say, because so far, the result has been significant loss for me.***

*'Father, I want to be well. I want to have a close personal relationship with you and be who you have called me to be. These things seem difficult to me and a long way off, but I ask you to meet me where I am – lost and stuck, tired, injured, emotionally scarred and physically weary. I am not in my right mind, as I struggle with depression, anxiety and stress. In your great mercy, could you please do a work in me and transform my mind, and my whole being? I surrender to you again and choose life today. Please meet me, Lord.'*

### 2nd March 2023

*Reading in 1 Samuel about the transition from Saul as king to David. I realised that God appoints and anoints to fulfill his purposes. God can give and remove his anointing as he chooses. Disobedience leads to removal. Obedience leads to victory, favour and blessing. It was also obvious that the blessings abound when God is near. In honest reflection, I am probably more like Saul than I would care to admit. I have had the anointing to build and to lead but am not sure if this still rests with me. I have to work hard to not compare my performance as CEO when I look at Jack and how well he is progressing. I am feeling more and more disconnected and it is becoming challenging for me to avoid frustration, maintain focus on what I have rather than what I have lost and resist playing the comparison game.*

***My lack of obedience to the Lord is having a sustained impact. Trying to do things my way has not worked.*** *God has been speaking but I have continually relied on my capacity and tried to prove myself, to myself and to others. Even through this recovery, I have tried to be productive and achieve my way through.* ***Surrender is difficult because the flesh has nothing else – just the importance of self. If this importance is removed, what am I? What have I achieved? What have I done? Who am I?***

*Unfortunately, my motivation for work is currently as low as it has ever been. In all this time, until now, I have never truly considered not returning to the role or my full capacity. I have never considered leaving the company, but I have recently realised that this decision might not be in my hands.*

***Honestly, I am just trying to get through to LSL and be moderately useful.*** *This is not what I consider giving my best to the company, but I just have no more in the tank. I don't have the energy, the drive, or the passion. In some ways, I have lost my sense of purpose. I feel like God is continuing to strip any capacity I have to contribute to my future or to plan my way out of this. Father God, I have nothing left. I need your help.*

### 9th March, 2023

*Yvette and I discussed my complete lack of motivation and she put it to me that perhaps I was beginning to accept the situation. The most exciting thing for me was that it appeared as though the Beast was not driving my choices. I felt no drive or desire to be there or to do more. This left me able to choose what I did and how I did it, and this is where the positive feelings have come from.*

*It throws up many other questions such as what I will do on return from LSL? But I am now free to engage or disengage as I see fit, and as required. I do not "have" to do anything. I don't need to operate out of a "should" to prove myself or meet some demand. Just choose how I am going to serve and do that. If I run out of batteries – go home.*

### 14th March, 2023

*Well, Well, Well!* ***It seems like things are changing and it is becoming a little exciting.*** *I am very cautious about getting too excited, knowing that* things can and have changed dramatically before. However, in the last week and a half, I have woken up with energy. I have not felt this way for at least the past two years. It has been a long time. Even after a long day, a hard workday and even back-to-back efforts, I have still woken up well with energy and a sense of positivity towards the day and all that comes my way. On top of that, the mental battle seems to have ceased, or at least eased. I am not tired from the relentless battle of overthinking and analysing every thought and action. I feel as though I am in a much better place. A place of acceptance.

**'Thank you, Lord, for this journey and for drawing me closer to you.** Thank you for correcting some of my misunderstandings. Please continue to reveal where I need a more accurate picture of the truth and help me have a closer relationship with you.

Thank you, Lord!!'

### 21st March 2023

Over the last couple of weeks, I have had considerably more energy and have also had a much healthier mindset and attitude. My level of self-awareness has increased dramatically and I am acutely aware of subtle changes in my physical state, and my mental state.

I am conscious of walking with and listening to God and I really want to hear what he has to say. I am aware of my habit of not journalling as much when things are going well. My actions reflect my independent and self-driven nature.

'Father, forgive me for remaining at arm's length and not seeking a closer relationship with you. Please reveal your thoughts towards me and help me listen to you.

*Father God, I need you to light my darkness. Shine your light on the deepest corners of my heart so that it can wash away my sins, and so that I can wholeheartedly serve you. Lord, also shine your light on my path, that I might know where to go and what to do.'*

### 29th March 2023

*My energy levels have remained high and my mental state is really quite positive. I have handled long days, crowds, even not minding hanging around at church for a little while. I have been able to let things go quickly at work and not pick up the responsibility that is not currently mine to handle. This is all good, and a welcome relief compared to the journey of the past couple of years.*

*I am still working through my picture of the Lord and my personal relationship with him. The message I am learning now is that God is much nicer than I think and desires a close relationship. He is a God of love and mercy and compassion.*

# PART 4

---

## END GAME

## CHAPTER 9
# THE CEO'S LAST STAND

After almost a month of newfound energy, a sense of freedom and a slowly building excitement about the future, perhaps unsurprisingly everything went wrong again. The CEO's last stand was a series of battles throughout the first three months of 2023, and it started on day one.

The CEO, whom I had now realised was a false identity, did not want to relinquish control. He had been running the show since my early childhood and every event in my life had served to build his system of beliefs, values, rules, and order. His offsider, the Beast, was perhaps the most brutal partner of this identity and they were hellbent on doing everything they could to regain control and put everything back in order, just the way it was. The CEO was clever and would not let a title imposed by others deter him from who he was. Stripped of the official CEO title, he simply embraced the new title of Executive Director. This could be even better. After all, directors operate at a higher level, a strategic and visionary level. With this title, the CEO might very well be unstoppable. Could this be a new birth for the CEO, a whole new chapter of perfectionistic overachievement fuelled by workaholism?

The anxiety associated with the unanswered "what if" questions around my return after long service leave was reaching fever pitch. I did not want to be overseas on leave and stressed about returning to work. Imagine sitting in a restaurant on Italy's Amalfi coast and thinking about the task ahead. What if, instead of enjoying the majesty of the Swiss Alps, I was mentally preparing for more appointments with the doctor and psychologist? What if, instead of immersing myself in Parisian culture, I was trying to unpack what my role might look like moving forward? What if I still had not recovered? What if I needed more time? What if, what if, what if?

The CEO, or should I say the newly titled Executive Director, seized this anxiety-driven opportunity and shifted into overdrive. After almost a month of near zero impact on my well-being and mental state, a new plan was afoot. The Executive Director saw an opportunity to wrestle back full control of my identity and my future. The plan was simple, and potentially very effective and involved writing a letter to the Board and asking them to put some firm options on the table. "Let's be mature about this and sort things out before I leave," I thought. Although the letter to the Board was open and transparent, I was once again acting in complete harmony with the CEO, sorry, the Executive Director and did not hold back on just how good the month of March had been. 'I felt like I was back' and I wanted the Board to know it. All that was needed now was for the Board to agree to either an easing back into my old role as CEO, or to clarify the parameters of my role as the Executive Director. I even asked for all changes to be in writing and a new contract to be written. Although I pushed my case in this letter, out of integrity and trust in them, the letter also left the decision to the Board.

Writing an open letter to the Board of Directors about your own future is a daunting proposition. The open-ended possibilities of their decisions are an uncomfortable reality. So, as the Executive Director, I took charge. I am an Executive Director. I know exactly what options they will put on the table, and once again I, Darren, in complete harmony with the Executive Director, went about writing my own response to the letter I had given to the Board.

In my response, I devised no less than seven alternative options, ranging from a gradual return on the same kind of plan I was currently following through to a full and immediate return to my old role, or new role. It also included some painful options, such as resignation, but I only put this down as a token option, not because I thought it might be a genuine possibility. I calculated hours, remuneration, work schedules and drafted a new set of responsibilities and KPIs. The Executive Director was loving it, he was living the dream.

As you might have guessed, because of this exercise, my mental health took a dramatic downward turn over the next couple of weeks. The anxiety in my chest burned with a new intensity. No amount of rubbing my sternum, or taking deep breaths, could ease the sensation, and nothing could stop the onslaught of negative thoughts and "what if" questions. It genuinely felt like I was all the way back at square one. I was not sleeping well, constantly worried about things and I did not want to be around anyone. Just get me out of here!

I thought I had dealt with all this nonsense. I had two sessions with Virgil in April and did not look forward to either of them. During the first session, in his typically honest fashion, he told me to go back and read page one of the "Happiness Trap," book. *Darren, you need to accept this. You need to let go. This is called dying to self. This is what Jesus did for you on the cross. The only way through is to let go, to surrender. Follow His lead. Accept reality, let go, surrender…"*

Instead, I organised a meeting with the Chair of the Board, Chris, to put my case forward in person. We had been friends since I was 15 years old, and I had been responsible for him becoming a board member. He was my biggest supporter, confidant, and mentor. Surely, he could see the incredible improvement and help me create a positive way forward. But he was kind of nervous and unsure about the meeting and my purpose in it.

We talked candidly, but delicately, about the future, but we did not address the specifics of the letter at all. Something was up!

I made no journal entries in April, which would normally be a sign that things were going well. However, on this occasion, it was the complete opposite. I was smack bang in the middle of the land of denial. My mental state was spiralling, sliding, falling back into the thick slimy pit of despair, depression, stress and anxiety and I could not handle it. There was no way out. I thought I had done this part of the journey. How could I have been so foolish? How could I be all the way back here again? And in the middle of it all, there was one exceptionally loud voice.

The CEO, or newly titled Executive Director, was making one last stand to regain control of my thoughts, my life, and my identity. He knew he had nearly killed me over the past two and a half years but did not care. He was now dangling the same carrot of self-righteous, perfectionist, workaholic success. He wasn't just whispering the future to me; he was screaming, ranting, and raving: Don't quit, keep fighting. This is how winning is done. Work, work, work, prepare, plan, adjust, work, fight, fight, fight... Darren, become the Executive Director, give yourself over completely to the work, the drive, and the pursuit of success. You are so close. Look at everything you have done and achieved. You can not only do it again, but you will do it bigger and better than ever before. With this experience under your belt, you will be unstoppable. You have all the skills you need, just commit to the process, do the work, set the goals, write the plan, learn whatever you have to, drive, work and smash the KPIs out of the park. Come on Darren, be all you were meant to be, be more than the CEO, be the Executive Director!

Perhaps, as I alluded to in a previous chapter, the CEO was echoing the words of the evil emperor Palpatine in Star Wars, "Darren use your drive, embrace the fight, make your journey to the dark side complete and fulfill your destiny."

## REFLECTION

### Leadership Lessons

- Fear is a powerful driver, but it is not always productive
  - Check your motives
- If you ask a question, you have to allow for the answer
  - If you only want one response, you will likely be disappointed
- Written clarity is always important
- Titles create energy and momentum
  - This can be good or bad
  - Be careful of the titles you seek and assign

For me, the CEO's last stand was an extremely intense battle for control of my soul, and my identity, and I didn't see it coming. There was simply no way this false identity was going to relinquish control without a fight. On a base level as humans, we don't like change. We like things the way they are or the way they have always been. This is our flesh, our sin nature. It likes comfort and ease. It does not like new, uncontrolled realities, especially when these new realities affect our livelihoods. The flesh does not want to relinquish control to God. This is the part of every person that rebels and fights against the Creator. This is the essence of the devil's pride, thinking and believing that it knows better than God. The flesh loves to use fear as a motivation for gaining control.

Are there any areas in your life where fear is the primary motivator?

How is this fear affecting your actions, your role, your leadership?

What do you need to do to let go of fear and control?

# CHAPTER 10

# SURRENDER

I don't think it is any coincidence that I read Bono's book "Surrender" over the 2022 - 2023 Christmas holidays. I have always loved U2's music and admired how they have been able to move with the times and connect with their audience over multiple generations. Their sound is completely unique, and their lyrics are insightful and provocative. Although I knew Bono was a man of faith, I did not know just how genuine his faith was and how he has worked to live it through his music, his politics, and his social and economic projects and endeavours. While his life hasn't been perfect and there are things I'm sure he would do differently, one thing that really caught my attention was his capacity to live in the present time of "not yet". He could see problems, feel heartache and witness need in every corner of the earth. He could engage in genuine change efforts and influence the most powerful people on the planet to provide exceptional levels of funding and support. However, he lived in the reality that whatever he achieved, it was and is rarely enough. Perhaps one of U2's most famous songs captures this capacity perfectly, *"I still haven't found what I'm looking for"*. This is what surrender is all about - both his book, and what's required to fully surrender to God. Knowing that God will work all things together for the good of those who love him. However, this understanding does not mean it will all be sunshine and roses. Living life surrendered to God is a process, not a destination. The process can be extremely challenging and forces us to come to terms with our present reality while believing in the substance of our preferred future. It's a process that forces us to face God. To face our demons. To choose to follow a path and live the consequences.

## EASTER HOLIDAYS 2023

"I am completely exhausted. I am done. I have nothing left to give. I have no more fight left in me." It is hard to explain the depths of despair and desperation I felt as the holidays began, and Good Friday approached. We had just under three weeks until departing on our scheduled long service leave. My wife and I had dreamed about this trip for years. We had been busy planning for about nine months, researching things to do and see throughout Europe. We had a lingering hope of enjoying some well-earned rest, taking the time for reflection, and just maybe experiencing some level of restoration and recovery.

As Good Friday approached, I turned to the Lord. Everything I had ever thought or believed and lived was inaccurate, inadequate or an out-and-out lie. Darren had totally ceased to exist and had truly become the CEO, or the Executive Director as he now liked to be called. I read through the biblical account of Jesus' journey up to and including his terrible crucifixion, and slowly, very slowly, I began to see clearly, perhaps for the first time in my life.

Jesus, the Son of God, willingly surrendered every fibre of his being to the will of His Father. He had lived a sinless life, a perfect life, listening to and obeying his father in heaven. And Father God was pleased with him. Jesus was God incarnate. The perfect representation of God. And in this moment, he laid all of that down and surrendered to His Father and obeyed him, even to the point of death on a brutal Roman Cross.

Now fortunately, we know the end of the story. We know that on the third day, Jesus conquered death and hell and rose again, and we know that 40 days later, he ascended into heaven. A further 10 days later, on the day of Pentecost, the promised Holy Spirit descended on the disciples in the upper room with power and tongues of fire and they set about changing the world with the message of the cross and salvation through Jesus. But the truth remains, **Jesus had to walk through the pain. He had to let go of everything he was, and everything he would ever be, or could ever be. He had to surrender his Godhood, and his humanity, and he had to trust His Father. The one and only person with a claim to the throne of the universe surrendered his life to the will of His Father and went through hell in the process.**

The Father's will for all of mankind to be reconciled to him has not changed since sin entered the world through the fall of Adam. Believing in the death and resurrection of his son Jesus and accepting him into our hearts as our personal Lord and Saviour is the path of reconciliation. When we truly walk this path, the scriptures come to life. We are made in his image, and it is no longer we who live, but Christ who lives through us.

As I read through this incredible story of sacrificial love, it dawned on me slowly...

### I need to follow Jesus' example!

There is only one choice. I have tried all that I know; I have fought and fought and fought. The game is over. I need to repent of living a lie and surrender and obey the Father. I need to surrender my life, my whole self, my flesh, my desires, my dreams, my ambitions, and my identity. In simple terms, **I need to die to self - the CEO needs to die at the foot of the**

**cross.** Darren needs to repent and surrender to the Father and be obedient to His will.

Genuine life can never happen without death coming first. Jesus repeatedly taught this message through many parables and if you read both the Old and the New Testament, you will see countless examples demonstrating the principle of death before life; sowing before reaping; submission before blessing and Jesus' life, death and resurrection is the ultimate example of this process. But it doesn't stop there. In Ephesians 4:22–24, we're encouraged to "put off the old self, which is being corrupted by its evil desires, to be made new in the attitude of your minds, and to put on the new self, created to be like God in true righteousness and holiness." And this is exactly where I was. I needed to put off the CEO. In my words, **I needed to "kill the CEO".** There was and is no other choice. Death was and is and always will be the path to life.

## JOURNALLING AND PAINTING

Throughout this journey, I have found two things that have significantly helped me to process and bring revelation direct from God. One of those is journalling, writing my thoughts out, warts and all. This has been a very cathartic process, albeit a little disturbing at times. The second is painting. I never knew I could paint, but my children inspired me as they all have wonderful artistic ability. Whilst I am no Picasso, I have really enjoyed it and found it incredibly useful. Beginning on Good Friday and through until Sunday, I painted the picture in my head. I could see it vividly and felt an incredible urge to paint what I saw and tell the story of my journey towards surrender.

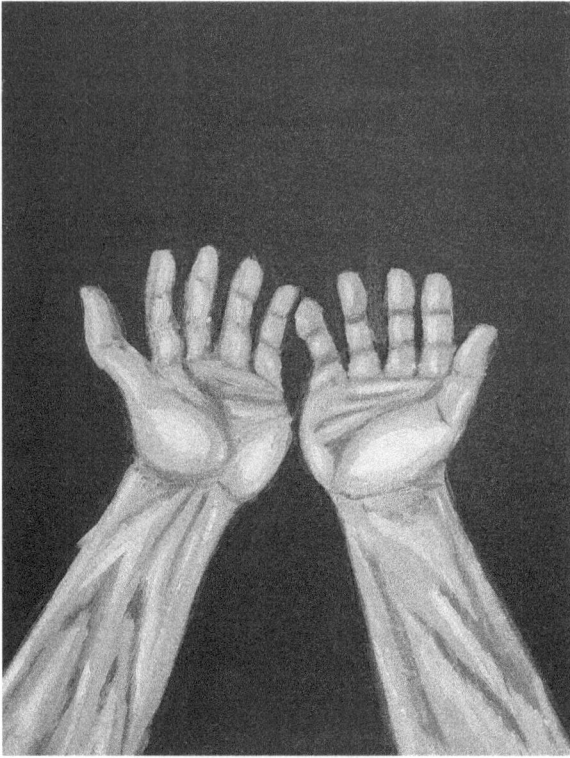

**10. My Surrender Hands**

## MY SURRENDER HANDS

In processing the meaning of this painting with my wife, Yvette, my best explanation was that this journey had felt like it had been a very, very long Good Friday. The fight, the battle, the wounds and scars and mental damage had all taken their toll, and it was still not enough. It was now time for me to surrender. This day had been a long time coming, and this act of surrender included everything. My work, my role, and my financial future.

It included my wellbeing, personal and professional relationships, dreams, goals, ambitions, strengths, and yes even my titles. My capacity, skills, abilities, gifts, deficiencies and lack all had to be surrendered. I even had to surrender my family, my wife, my sons, and my daughter. Literally, no area of my life was left un-surrendered.

Until this very moment of surrender, I had no other picture of the future in my mind. My intention was to be in this role, serving God until the day I died. I knew what I thought were the God-given plans for the company, its future direction, and expansion. My dream was not only for this company. This dream and these plans encapsulated everything I was or ever hoped to be. But the dream was over. I had to surrender everything. I did not know what the future held. All I could picture was a gigantic black chasm of the unknown. I had to trust God.

Throughout my life, I had tried to control everything, and the false identity of the CEO fully believed that ultimately, he was in control of everything. My letter to the Board the week prior was my, or should I say our, last ditch effort to control what was on the other side of long service leave. If you like, **the CEO and I were trying to control what would happen on the other side of the grave. Not even Jesus did that!**

## KILLING THE CEO

So, on completion of the painting and through my discussion with Yvette, I surrendered to the Lord, and this was my prayer:

*"Lord, I have nothing left. I surrender everything to you. As you can see, I have nothing to give you. My hands are empty. Without you, I can do nothing. Without you, I am nothing. Please forgive me Lord, for I am the chief of sinners. I have lived in arrogant self-righteousness, pride, and deception. My 'Self', my 'Flesh', the 'CEO' has been in control, driving me to feed the Beast, and to serve itself. I have been living a lie, believing that I am the CEO, believing that*

*I am in control of everything. Father, right now I surrender this false identity, this false reality to you. I give you all my hopes and dreams. I give you my life. I am yours Father. From this point forward, I lay down and surrender my life to you. Not my will, Lord, but yours. I surrender."*

When I finally came to the point of admitting that I am nothing and have nothing to give to God, I had quite the revelation. **God does not need me!** Can you get your head around that? **I am not necessary!** God is the king of the universe and can do whatever he pleases. He does not need me to achieve His will. ***But Grace upon Grace upon Grace–God wanted me in His world. He had a thought, and a plan and chose to create me. He led me along a path to this moment where I would become fully submitted to Him so he could achieve his plans in and through me. Wow! Just wow!***

## VICTORY

Spiritually, we know Jesus didn't just lie around in the tomb and wait for Sunday. The will of his Father was complete restoration and reconciliation of mankind to himself. In obedience, Jesus descended into the depths, took the keys of death and hell and defeated Satan once and for all. And on Sunday he rose victorious. He rose as the Christ; the Messiah appearing to hundreds of people over the next 40 days before ascending into heaven to be seated at the right hand of the Father. But he did not stop there. He sent the Holy Spirit to dwell inside every believer to be our helper and to provide wisdom and guidance and to draw all men to himself.

The rest of the weekend felt amazing. I felt light. Tired, but light. Light in heart and light in spirit. To continue the Easter analogy, I was enjoying Saturday, and in some ways, I still am. Resting in the truth that the CEO was no more, and even more than that, I am no more. My life is not my own. I belong to Jesus, who lives in me. I am a new creation. **I am born again!**

## RELEASE

Time was pressing and I had arranged a meeting with the Board on the Wednesday morning at 10am. This was decision day. I had asked the Board to put some firm options on the table so we could all be confident of the process moving forward. On Tuesday night, after the Easter weekend, Yvette and I were discussing what might happen at this meeting. I had surrendered everything to God and Yvette was right beside me. We were united in our thinking and in our surrender. Nervous, but united. I remember saying very clearly to her, "Whatever happens, I am just really looking forward to the release."

As I entered the meeting, there was a sense of formality that I was not really expecting. I had very close relationships with each of the Board members, but they were professional and had a job to do. Although they were 100% supportive of me and wanted the best for my long-term health, they had a company to run. They had a legal and moral obligation to ensure that the leader of the company was fit for duty. As requested, they provided me with just two written options. Nothing like the seven options that I had drafted behind the scenes. And in the end, the choice was simple. The Board believed in me and did not want to sack me. I believed in the organisation and did not want to resign. However, we were all in agreement that I was no longer fit for the role of CEO, and it was unknown if I would ever have that capacity again. So, I chose the option put before me. Perhaps ironically, the legal term for the document used was called a "Deed of Release". Can you believe that? Even in the most difficult of circumstances for me, God had gone before and provided written confirmation of the choice that had to be made.

Allow me to pause here for a moment and recap the significance of this battle and just what was on the line.

## IF THE CEO WINS, I DIE.

The result of the CEO running my life and trying to meet his expectations could well have led to physical death. The depths of depression, peaks of anxiety and the burn of stress could all have ended in physical death. These, when combined with the dangerous habits of self-medication, poor diet, lack of exercise, and a lack of sleep, seriously increase this possibility.

If I did not die physically, and the CEO won the battle, I would be stuck forever living a false reality. Working harder and longer with less satisfaction. The CEO's appetite for success would enslave me, driving me to perfection and focusing on whatever was next. Satisfaction for a job well done or a task complete would never be realised. I would become a shell of my former self, my true self, all the while believing I was serving God and being the best I could be.

## IF DARREN WINS, I LIVE ... I GET MY LIFE BACK.

If I win, I discover, or perhaps rediscover, who Darren is. And I get the joy of becoming the best version of myself in every facet of my life. I am free to just be me and do whatever I choose. If I win, the CEO becomes a life-filled experience with lessons and wisdom that can help release me into a much healthier future.

If I win, I might just find God and my true self. I might begin to live a life of abundance reflecting my true identity as someone who is loved by God and chosen to partner with him in bringing the Kingdom of Heaven to reality here on earth.

Want some great news? I surrendered, The CEO and I die, God Wins, and I am free.

**Darren is born again!**

# REFLECTION

**Leadership Lessons**

- Living in the present time of "not yet" is a genuine tension that every leader must learn to manage
- The greatest leader in history was the greatest follower
- The greatest act of leadership is to follow Jesus' example
  - To live a life of surrendered obedience to the Father
- Taking time to reflect and express your thoughts and feelings in different ways can lead to revelation
  - Invest in yourself
  - Give yourself permission

Pause and consider this truth:

**God Does not need you. He chose you and invited you to work with him on his plans.**

Will you surrender to God today?

What would it look like if you truly surrender and allow Christ to live through you? How would this change your life?

# CHAPTER 11

# BECOMING DARREN

## RELEASE, FREEDOM, RESTORATION, LIFE!

A t the end of April 2023, Yvette and I flew out to Europe for our long-awaited long service leave, and we were completely free. Again, I felt light, as if someone had lifted a massive weight off my shoulders. A load that I had been carrying for years was no longer there and we were free to embrace this holiday for what it was, the trip of a lifetime. We could now fully choose to do as much or as little as we wanted and just engage, relax, embrace, and enjoy. I was no longer driving myself with "shoulds" or internal expectations of achievement or trying to portray a particular image that I was never meant to be. And despite having no job to return to, and no future income, I simply did not have a worry in the world. I knew God had all things under control and that I could now completely trust him. I just had to enjoy being Darren.

This trip was incredibly important for both Yvette and me. It was the longest time we had holidayed on our own since we were married 28 years prior. Since having our four kids, the longest we had been away on our own was a week. So, to be on the other side of the world for 11 weeks, just the two of us was a whole new level of special. It was very restorative. We had time to laugh, to reflect, to enjoy and embrace. We had the time and the space to engage with the culture and live every moment. This felt like a true reward from the Lord. A very generous gift. All the while, the Lord was gently talking to us, leading, guiding and providing for us. He spoke to us individually and together and we could just feel his life pulsing through our veins. There were a few days throughout the trip where fatigue kicked in and reminded me that recovery from such an intense burnout journey will take some time. But by God's grace and leading, we had prepared for this. We had at least one day in every location designated for rest – and I needed it.

## STAYING IN THE PRESENT

When you have been through a journey like mine, it's impossible not to think forwards occasionally. And if you let your mind run too far ahead, it's not long before you experience a heightened sense of anxiety. This occurred several times, and if I am honest, it still happens today. Fortunately, I've become more aware of my thoughts and how my body reacts to them, so I can recognise what's going on and adjust as required. This heightened experience is especially noticeable when I am doing something new, or something I have not done for quite some time. For example, re-engaging in the social space, particularly at church, took some courage. I felt the anxiety rising immediately and only after I noticed it was I able to identify why my chest was burning again. It wasn't bad; it wasn't some pending doom. It was just my body preparing for a previously threatening situation. Awareness and a deliberate choice to let those thoughts pass by were the key to handling the situation more easily than I had in the past. I am reminded of a passage of scripture in Matthew 6: 25 – 34 where we are repeatedly encouraged not to worry. Verse 34 specifically says, "Therefore do not worry about tomorrow, for tomorrow will worry about itself. Each day has enough trouble of its own." As Virgil would often remind me, there is no pain in the present, so stay present. When we look backwards, it is easy to get depressed. When we focus too far forward, anxiety increases, but the truth is God gives us the grace we require for right now. His mercies are new every morning, and his grace is sufficient for me and for you.

## INCREASED AWARENESS

The first and most important part of leadership is leading self, and the first step in self-leadership is self-awareness. Acute awareness of how my body reacts to different stressors and triggers has been a significant key for me in proactively choosing my responses. I am no longer held hostage by a false identity that condemns and shames and drives and pushes. The CEO always reacted. Any threat was a threat to his control and his grip on my identity. So, this increased level of self-awareness has been an incredibly powerful tool to guide my responses and my choices and enabled me to live free and to be Darren.

## NEW ANCHORS AND FRESH REVELATIONS

During the trip, God used some special moments and locations to create new anchors for me. Vivid, concrete examples of his character and capacity. We would visit ancient cities and churches and would marvel at the majesty of the Swiss Alps. We immersed ourselves in the culture and the arts, embracing the opportunity for such convenient travel. We would enjoy medieval cities, stay in 600-year-old castles, visit incredible coastlines, swim in the Mediterranean and enjoy cocktails on the rocky beaches. We just happened to be in Monaco–Monte-Carlo, one of the wealthiest places on earth, in the week of the Monaco Grand Prix. The elite of the elite live here or visit for occasions such as this. Looking down at the marina, you can see multi-million-dollar vessels filled with absolutely everything money can buy. Every second car was a Lamborghini, a Ferrari, a Porsche, Rolls Royce, or Bentley; if you could name an exotic car, it was there. In the middle of it all, God gave me quite a simple but powerful revelation.

**"The very best man can do in all his attempts to show his greatness is to drive the fanciest vehicle to stay in the fanciest location, to admire what God has made!"**

Can you get your head around that? No matter where we went, this revelation rang true. Standing in the Alps, it did not matter if I had skis and snow gear or jeans and a t-shirt; the majestic snow-covered mountain range was God's creation. The placement of the stars in the sky is incomprehensible to me, yet God did this. Man has travelled to the moon. Wow, a truly incredible achievement! But he didn't make the moon. Sitting on the rocky beach in Nice sipping cocktails and enjoying the quiet peacefulness that is the Mediterranean, it was impossible to distinguish where the ocean stopped, and the sky began. Man struggles to paint this, let alone create it. Not only that, but I could sit on this beach trusting that the tide would not go beyond its preset limits. God set these limits when he divided land from water. No man has made an ocean. No man has made oxygen; in fact, no man has created something from nothing. Yes, man is creative because he is made in the image of God. However, every single creative exploit of man has used the materials that God created. The very best we can do is to enjoy what he has made.

As I sat there pondering this profound revelation,  He simply said to me, **"I've got this."** Wow, what peace! What encouragement! No striving required. No worry needed. Faith - yes, but worry - no. The God of the universe was personally reminding me, that he is big. If he is big enough to create the universe, then he is big enough to take care of me. And perhaps one of the sweetest parts of this revelation, was that he was personal.

He was talking to me about my situation. "Darren, I've got this." I have reminded myself of this so many times since he first spoke to me. It always takes the focus off me and what I can do and puts the responsibility fairly and squarely on his shoulders. My only task if you like is to let go and trust him. The CEO would never have been able to understand this. The false identity of the CEO was convinced that he was in control of all things. And while he theoretically believed in God, the CEO had set himself up as the supreme being, in control and responsible for everything. It was so good, such a relief to be discovering the truth of being Darren. Created by God, for God.

## BECOMING A JOURNEY MAN

As I have shared throughout this book, the CEO had taken over my life and was determined to "**get there**" wherever "there" may be; the other side of the tracks? The CEO was always destination focused, but ironically never satisfied. As a result, I found that my experience of joy was limited and diminishing. Even when a project came together or a goal was achieved, the satisfaction would not last for long and would simply not satisfy the CEO's desire for success. For example, I remember captaining my local AFL team to a grand final victory and the euphoria of the victorious moment had passed for me before I left the field of play. It just didn't satisfy. I recall another time when the company had achieved its highest ever net profit, a goal we had been working for and was central in our plans to move forward. This did not even raise my eyebrows let alone my heart rate, or fill my soul with any sense of satisfaction. It only propelled me to work harder and do better next year. These examples were not insignificant, they required months, if not years of investment and leadership, and yet the focus on the destination always ended in a sense of dissatisfaction and a future focus on how to do better next time. When he was in control no matter how far I went on the journey, or how high I climbed, or what obstacles were overcome, or how well others followed my leadership it simply did not matter. Call it greed or pride, or false humility, call it whatever you like, the CEO was a destination man who did not care for the destination. There was only ever the pursuit of more. More work, more to do, faster, and better.

However, now that I was free to be Darren, I was loving the opportunity to look at things through a new set of lenses. It was almost as if I was experiencing real life for the first time. I could see God in everything, and I sensed the depth of his love for me. I was enjoying his provision and not trying to be anywhere or anyone else. I was loving it. Through God's grace, I was becoming a journey man rather than a destination man. I was moving with God in his direction, all the while feeling as though I was moving towards him, a little closer each day. My journal entries took on a whole new flavour while on this trip and as I looked at life through this new set of lenses, metaphors, direction, purpose, provision, care, concern and rest, you name it, God was speaking, and I was listening like never before.

This was not the first time I had pondered on the journey rather than the destination; however, it highlights again that I am somewhat of a slow, stubborn learner. I suspect that my slowness was an outworking of the false identity of the CEO refusing to embrace the journey or any kind of different approach. It simply did not fit with his psyche or his desire to get there. However, slowly but surely, I was being restored and beginning to feel alive again.

I not only had to agree with God and be willing to follow his lead, but this journey towards God required my wise participation. To be honest with you, even now as I'm writing, the journey is not over. Positive daily choices are still required, and I need to monitor my energy and capacity every day. Just because I have managed to kill the false identity that was the CEO, it does not mean that thoughts and desires won't return, and it doesn't mean all my thoughts, dreams and desires were bad. The process has been about surrendering these to God and letting him determine my steps. And because I have not been this way before – total trust and faith in God is required.

Being involved in outdoor education for more than 20 years, I have always admired the journey and embraced the challenge of expeditions and high intensity experiences. And one night while I was sitting on the balcony of our unit on the Amalfi coast, I felt God speaking to me metaphorically. He showed me the magnificent Italian coastline rising from the ocean to the mountain top. The rise was incredibly steep with cliffs and rocky out-crops, areas that were covered in thick, almost impassable vegetation and other areas that were open and exposed, and still other areas that were quite flat and calm. As I pondered what it would take to scale this mountainous coastline from the beach to the peak, I could picture the journey of life.

The beginning of the journey was a process of proving, testing and achievement; much like our journey as we finish school, enter the work-force, and forge our careers. About a third of the way up this coastline was a difficult rocky cliff section. It was steep and rugged and would require significant skill, grit, and endurance. To me, this spoke of that point in life where we really show our mettle, what we are made of and where we achieved some really impressive successes. For some, this might be a pro-motion, a title, or a major deal. Others might connect this to their finances, while others might link it to marriage and children. At this point on the coastline, there was a relatively flat area with a house, and I thought to myself, it would be a genuinely satisfying life calling to live in that house and help others reach that point.

However, the rest of the journey from this point looked exponentially more difficult and yet more rewarding. It would require a different type of person with a different mindset and a different skill set. Whereas the first section was all about proving self and achievement, this next section appeared impossible to traverse alone. It would require equipment and assistance. It would require other people to help you, and you to help other people. This section was not about pace or achievement. It was about perspective, good choices, care for others, wise leadership, and the wisdom to follow others. From this point to the very top of what I could see had a continuous flow of steep climbs and challenging descents. There was no physical way to jump from peak to peak, the journey would require the ups and the downs. It looked a little like the graph of the stock market if you like; constantly fluctuating but increasing over time. When I first looked at this rugged skyline, I considered the declines as further losses and failures, but this wasn't the message God was showing me now.

As I pondered some more, I realised that these areas were in fact areas of protection, rest, and safety. Although the peaks could be considered the achievements, they were short, sharp, and momentary. The lower points were absolutely necessary; they provided protection from direct exposure to the elements, the wind, the rain, and the sun. They provided a safe place to stop and refuel and reset your gear for the next climb. And perhaps most significantly, I realised that the perspective gained by scaling this mountain was never lost. Even when resting in a recess between peaks, the perspective gained was so much greater than any previous point on the journey.

## NEW PERSPECTIVES

The CEO was a false identity and had a completely inaccurate picture of the world. In the CEO's mindset, life was a journey from glory to glory. From peak to peak. There is no way the CEO could embrace a descent as anything other than a failure. It would not matter to the CEO how high the mountain was, to go down was to fail. But praise God, I was being transformed by a loving, personal God. I was now enjoying being Darren and reimagining the events of my life, and the events to come. I could see some of the potential dips in the road, but it didn't matter, I knew that God had put these in place for my good. Even as I write now, I am resting in a recess between peaks.

Work in my new business has currently halted. I know more will come in because God told me that he's got this. But the truth is the stress is incredibly real. The old self, the CEO, would have driven and pushed and pushed, ultimately without any substantive gains. In fact, from experience, pushing would have resulted in increased fatigue, depression, and anxiety. However, as I continue to operate from a transformed mindset, I realise that God has provided this downtime to complete this book and create a preferred future. In this recess, he has protected my time and my heart and allowed me to focus on first things first. Not only have I been able to focus on writing, but I have increased my exercise and begun to take control of my financial situation. I have had time to connect with family and friends and increase my commitment to the church. And in all of this I have found rest.

## UNDERSTANDING REST

Up until this point in my life, I have never understood the concept of rest. I know God rested on the seventh day and provided the sabbath for us to do the same. But honestly, I had no idea what rest was all about. It has only been through this journey that I discovered the essence of rest. By stopping for a moment, a day if you like, you take your hands off the steering wheel and your foot off the accelerator. You choose to stop and be reminded that you are not in control, God is. Resting in God is not an act of irresponsibly throwing your hands in the air like you just don't care. Resting in God is stopping yourself long enough to be quiet and still and trust that He has got this.

The questions don't go away. Thoughts, doubts, and fears will flow through your mind sometimes like a raging torrent, at least that is what happens for me. However, the important step here is to pause for a moment and consider, God is in charge of the raging river and where it is going. He is also in charge of the riverbanks and the trees and the plains and the valleys. He knows where you are, and he knows what you need. If God can meet me at the bottom of a mud filled slimy cesspool, burnt out, stressed, depressed, and consumed with anxiety. If he can remove me from a place of security in a title and living from a false identity to a place of peace and rest, then he can do the same for you. For the first time in my entire life, I am peaceful; I have rest in him.

## DISCOVERING DARREN

I am discovering, or perhaps rediscovering the real Darren. I am adventurous. I like to get outdoors and explore. I enjoy all things physical and have found new joy in mountain biking, bushwalking, and paddle boarding. However, I am no longer trying to beat anyone and everyone. I am just enjoying these activities because they are fun. Painting has been an important part of my journey and continues to provide joy and fulfilment. It is just really cool to express myself in a format where I am not highly skilled. It is not something I am trying to be better than anyone else at. If a painting works, then good. If it doesn't then it doesn't. It does not make me a good or a bad person, a success, or a failure. To learn is fun and I have noticed a returned passion for reading, learning and leading. Despite the daily frustrations and challenges of parenting adults, I have found that I am connecting with my children on a whole new level and in a whole new way. We are enjoying each other's sense of humour, and I am allowing them to be themselves. One big change is my capacity to let them rest, rather than push them to do something more productive with their time and their life. My wife and I have always been close, but I have even found a new capacity to engage and connect with her on a daily basis. I have even sensed an increase in my curiosity, care and concern for my family and friends. Where I had become quite inward focused, I am now beginning to expand my horizons and see the needs of others.

Perhaps the best part of this journey is not actually knowing what the end product will look like. While I am a big believer in planning and beginning with the end in mind, I have come to realise that it is not about the destination. It is about who I am. Or should I say whose I am? It has only been through my deepening and more honest relationship with the Lord that I have begun to discover my true self. Where once the picture in my head was of fists tightly clenched as if ready for a fight holding on to what I had created and achieved with everything I had, the picture has now changed. My hands are open with palms facing the sky, and it is as though God is saying, "you have done all you can do, now let me show you what I can do." And I have this incredible sense of expansive opportunities, not just for the here and now, but into the future, and eternity. You see, God is not limited to our concept of the future. God is eternal. The steel he is weaving into the fabric of our being is not just for us. It is not just for now. It is for his purposes and his glory. And in this light, I am excited to let God show me who Darren is and how to be the very best version of who he has called me to be.

## REFLECTION
**Leadership Lessons**

- Whatever you are doing – schedule rest into your calendar
- Become acutely aware of the physical signs in your body
  - Pause and reflect on these and then choose what to believe and do about these signs
- No one can match God
- God is big enough to handle everything and he cares enough to handle your problems
- Be a journey person, not a destination person
- Perspective gained is never lost
- Resting between the peaks is a place of safety, refreshing, protection and blessing
- Helping others succeed is a worthy life calling
- To rest is to trust God
- Choose what thoughts you will agree with
- Allow God to enable you to be your best self

Who are you? Take some time to identify the real you. Can you put it in writing? What do you believe? What are your likes, dislikes, strengths, and weaknesses? What do you love to do? What do you prefer not to do?

Think about the following areas and identify who you would be at your best in each of these:

Spiritual

Physical

Emotional

Social

Financial

Are there gaps between you now and your picture of yourself at your best? If so, how could you invite God to lead you towards being the best version of yourself?

# CHAPTER 12
# FAITH IN ACTION

## AGREEMENT WITH GOD

I have heard faith defined, in simple terms, as agreement with God. If God has made a promise, then it will be done. Look at the world and the universe. When God speaks, things happen. There is no possible way we just climbed up out of some cosmic ooze and began to create life in all its complexity. We also know that God cannot lie. He cannot deny his own character. So, faith is accepting that God is God, and that He kind of knows what he is doing. Who would have thought! Faith in action is to live this truth every day. To live in agreement with God every day.

The problem for us is that we don't see the world as it is! We see the world from our perspective; our tiny perspective. We cannot fathom the majesty of God and so our problems, well, they seem huge. We have immediate problems right here, right now in our world and we need his help. And we want his help our way. So, we pray and seek the Lord passionately with very specific prayers about our needs and sometimes God comes through the way we want. But then there are other times where our prayers go by seemingly unanswered or not answered the way we hoped. We can feel disappointed when we believe the outcome is not enough, not satisfactory, or, in the worst case, when there is no outcome at all. When this happens, it's easy for our faith to be damaged because the God of the universe has not responded to our prayers the way we wanted him to, or the way we told him to. And our response to his response, or lack thereof, is often not one of gratitude, but complaint, whining, questioning and unbelief. We just can't comprehend why such an all-knowing, all-powerful God would not or did not answer our prayers and do things our way.

Unfortunately, I have to admit that I have unwittingly lived much of my life out of agreement with God. That is, out of faith with the God of the universe. Throughout this journey, I have come to realise that I might better describe my faith as a faint hope. Sometimes, a very faint hope. I know he can heal. I've experienced it. I know he can provide. I have received provision. I know he has plans to prosper me and not to harm me. I have lived and continue to live a blessed life. And his word says that we are co-heirs with Christ with full access to the kingdom and I have lived much of life in the favour of God. But I still get stuck - I'm unsure if he will come through this time. I mean, this time I need real money... like yesterday! It is not called a cost-of-living crisis for no reason. And don't get me started on my need for healing.

In my world, living from the false and fused identity of the CEO, my perspective and needs nearly always appeared extremely urgent, important, and sometimes insurmountable. And battered by the lack of previous positive results, my faith has often felt as though it has been in a state of rapid freefall. So, to sadistically prove myself right, in harmony with the CEO, my pattern has been to pray a defeated prayer. That is to pray without believing God can or will do anything. You may know how this sounds… "Hey God, if you can, I need some help, but whatever, I know you are busy." I would then rattle off a reasonably pathetic wish list of nice things that I think might help, but I don't combine it with faith-filled agreement.

The truth is, when I pray like this, it reflects that I am not convinced that God will provide, or even want to provide and then I get disappointed. And I am now not too proud to admit that in some cases, I have basically given up all hope and accepted that my blessing was not in his overall plan. You can see how a false identity works every angle to drive a wedge between you and the Creator. For me, the CEO would use this type of prayer and subsequent non-results to prove that it was indeed up to him to provide. God was not required, just more hard work. It is only now that I am seeing life through a set of transformed eyes that I am learning to pray with faith and agreement with God.

Without realising it, I have been fooled by the lie of the prosperity doctrine and quietly hoped it would be true. You possibly know the following verses well. Luke 6:38 says, "Give and it will be given back to you. A good measure pressed down, shaken together, and running over will be poured into your lap..." Wow, who wouldn't want that? Give to God and He will give back. Outstanding! And John 10:10 says "... I have come that they may have life and have life to the full". Fantastic - the best of life, all the time. From glory to glory, right?... Well! Incidentally, the CEO loved the prosperity doctrine. It was the perfect belief system to encourage more work. Work to get, work to give, work to do more work.

But God is not a get rich quick scheme. He does not operate like a supermarket where you go in with your list, pay the right amount and you get what you want. Giving to get is an almost incomprehensible motive with which to approach God. Giving to get, puts me in the driver's seat. It suggests that I am the one in charge; I know what I need, and God needs to provide in accordance with what I have given. The giving to get motive is treating God like an ATM with an unlimited supply. It is the age-old method of bargaining. If I do this, then you do that. If I give you this, then you give me that. This mindset was central to the CEO's operating system.

**Newsflash folks, this is not how God operates.** He is God. He is in charge. And he is all knowing. His understanding of your need extends beyond your few minutes on earth. He sees you in the picture of eternity, and he knows what you need and when you need it. And despite his unfathomable majesty that is not confined by time, he still cares for you in this very moment, and he wants a personal relationship with you in the here and now. So, faith in action is not about bargaining with God, but trusting that he knows what you need and will provide that. It is a little embarrassing just how many times I have set the course for my life and made the plans and then asked God to bless them. Talk about out of line, and out of faith agreement with God. It is perhaps a little ironic that one of my favourite passages is in James 4:13–17, where we are given the very clear directive not to boast about our plans ahead of time, but we should say, "If it is the Lord's will, we will live and do this or that." Did you catch that? We can't even take a breath outside of the Lord's will, let alone dictate the plans for our lives. I sometimes struggle to realise just how stubborn and stupid I have been.

However, there is good news. Through this journey, my gradual change of perspective and the acceptance of reality, I can see clearly for the first time in my life. I am now a new creation, and my work is simply to believe; to have faith; to agree with God and follow his lead. My work is to step off the seat of judgement and decision and surrender to his will and trust him to lead, to guide and to provide. This is exceptionally hard when there is more money going out than there is coming in. As I said previously, our faith matters most when it directly affects our way of life and for me, not having sufficient income to cover the weekly cost of living is a critical issue. Watching your savings deplete on a weekly basis, all the while professing faith in God for provision is … well, challenging.

My distinct lack of capacity to work and control the outcome has compounded this precarious position. But this is what faith is - evidence of things not seen. Full surrender to God and full agreement with him. If you ever want to live life on the edge, come and sit next to me. It is only when we reach such a place that Christ is fully living in us and through us. And we know what he can do. The work I need to do daily is to make the choice to follow Christ's example of complete surrender and obedience to the Father. You will notice in my journal entries that I don't hide my struggle with God. It is real, and to deny that would be to deny reality. If I have learnt nothing else on this journey, acceptance of reality is the key to reducing the suffering. Remember the suffering equation; Expectation – Reality = Suffering. It also places my faith in God at the centre, not me and my capacity.

## ALIGNING MY MOTIVES WITH GOD'S WILL

Allow me to be practical for a moment. God has given me skills and abilities and expects me to use them. He expects me to do business and create wealth. The difference is in the motive. When the CEO was driving the ship, the motive was about title and identity and control. It was about working hard, feeding the Beast, and proving myself. I have lost none of the skills, wisdom, or understanding of how to do business or create wealth. If anything, my understanding has gone to a whole new level. The difference is that my purpose and trust are in God and doing His will. It is with this confidence that I can approach God and ask him to provide. He can then choose how he provides. He might provide the income through work, or he might provide another way. Work is not bad; it is required. It was part of God's plan before the fall, so we should not be afraid of it. In the story of Peter fishing on the lake, when Jesus told Peter to cast out on the other side of the boat in Luke 5: 4- 11, Peter was working at his trade. He fished for a living and had been out all night and caught nothing. He could well have responded to Jesus with frustration and sarcasm. But he followed his direction. He let the nets down on the other side of the boat and hauled in a mighty catch. Similarly, when we read the parable of the talents in Matthew 25: 14 - 30, it is safe assume that the first two men who doubled their talents, went to work, and used their skills, their business savvy, to create the increase. The third man was deemed wicked because he concealed his talents and did not produce any advantage for his master. Further still, we learn Paul used his tent making skills to fund his missionary journeys as he spread the gospel (Acts 18: 1 - 4). Work is a good thing. To do business is a good thing and this, by the grace of God, is what I am now doing.

However, faith in action is not the same as being a fool in action. As a diagnosed workaholic, I need some strong boundaries in place. In our own company, my wife and I have written a policy into the founding document that neither we nor anyone employed by us will work more than four days a week. This is not a legal thing, or just a pleasant idea, but a boundary to stop me from feeding the Beast and burning out again. This is a deliberate policy that will ensure that I have time for work, rest, and play. And I can tell you in all honesty, I am loving it. The freedom to down tools on a Friday and just do whatever I choose is a genuine pleasure. Not only that, but my faith is that God will provide for all our needs in the four days that I work. **Isn't it strange how our greatest freedom and greatest peace comes from the tightest parameters?** But wait, there is still more. Recently, despite my best efforts to live in agreement with God, the flow of work has ground to a halt. Upon reflection, this has not been about God's lack of care or favour or provision, but his absolute care, favour, and provision. The CEO's old patterns of behaviour, which I am still prone to adopt, reflect a belief that I am responsible to fix this situation. However, God is saying again, "Darren, rest, I've got this." Scripture tells us that Paul asked God to remove the thorn from his flesh, but God only answered by saying, "My grace is sufficient for you" 2 Corinthians 12: 7 - 10. I wonder if the flow of provision depends directly on my ability to live in agreement, with full faith and trust in God? I wonder if this is a tool the Lord is using to help me stay close to him?

## LIFE TO THE FULL

Another passage that I have previously misunderstood is John 10:10, which states that "I have come to give life and life to the full", or life in abundance, as some manuscripts say. This is such an amazing encouragement and anchor for many, and it has been this for me. However, I must admit again that my perception has not been entirely accurate. My basic understanding of this verse is that we go from glory to glory, from strength to strength, not just life, but life to the full! As I was reflecting over this journey, the Lord showed me quite gently that there is more to it. Let me explain. We often hear the statement that death is just part of life, and as Christians, we should not fear death because we know we will reign with Christ for all eternity. But as I reflected on this passage a little more, the Lord revealed that life encompasses more than just all the good bits. **The struggles are part of the fullness of life. The depths of depression, the intensity of the fatigue of burnout, the stress and burden of responsibility, the desperation of complete lack, the burn of anxiety, the pain of lost love and relationships, the wounds of grief and loss can all be part of this full life.**

When Jesus says he came to bring life and life to the full, he was not saying that we would all live happily and easily ever after. **He promised we would experience life in all its fullness. That is; the good, the bad and sometimes the ugly,** and that it was how we engaged with the fullness of life that would reveal his work in our life. Our lived example would be the true testimony of our lives.

Being a person of faith does not exclude you from the trials of life. It certainly hasn't excluded me from this journey. Being a person of faith presents you ready and empowers you to engage all of life with hope and assurance. We only discover what we really believe when we are truly tested. And if our faith is true, then God gets the glory because it is at that point that he gets to decide what happens next. Once we stop trying to do God's work for him, or telling him how to do it, only then can he open our eyes to the possibilities and opportunities all around us. I have spent the last couple of years arguing with God, fighting with him, pleading with him to get me out of this pit, this bog, this muddy hole. But he has simply walked through the pit with me. And it possibly won't surprise you that in the process, he has opened my eyes to the pain of others around me.

Once again, in brutal honesty, I must admit that I can be quite superficial. It is a well-worn path of self-protection that I employ often – particularly in crowds and I am sad to say, especially at church. This superficiality was demonstrated in a lack of compassion and an active avoidance of in-depth conversations with others. The CEO's pattern of behaviour included keeping relationships at arm's length so as not to get too involved or entwined in someone else's troubles. It also included any action that would protect the CEO's reputation and position. However, things are slowly beginning to change.

As I have begun to live from my true identity, simply as Darren, I have noticed the needs around me. Recently at church I noticed the body language of a mate. I just knew something wasn't quite right. So, I did something quite rare and called him later that afternoon. We met for a glass of wine, and he shared just how much he had been struggling with his mental health and a level of physical burnout. Can you believe this? I knew what this guy was going through, and now I knew how to talk with him and even how to help him. And better yet, we have continued to connect regularly to ensure he has an avenue for discussion, processing, and support. To be honest, the conversations have been just as useful for me as well. Who would have thought that my pain and prolonged battle would empower me to be used by God to meet someone else at their point of need?

So, faith in action for me is to accept every aspect of my life and my experiences as a gift from the Lord. He truly has given me life to the full. Faith in action is to be grateful for life and to seek him. It is to ask him how he wants me to use my gifts, abilities, and experiences to walk in relationship with someone else facing a similar trial. Faith is following the Lord with my eyes and ears open, looking for opportunities to meet the needs of others. Faith in action even includes creating a way to do business, to create increase and to be a faithful steward. Friends, this is God's plan. Putting our faith into practical action is how we can stand in agreement with Paul in Galatians 2:20 and say that "it is no longer I who lives, but Christ who lives in me." We are his instruments of grace, of healing, of provision. We receive the blessing of living life to the full, not for our glory or title or money, but so we can connect with others on their journey and reflect and reveal Christ to them.

Faith in action is a journey of surrender and a process of continual transformation. While the gift of salvation is never revoked, we are implored by Paul in Philippians 2:12-13, to "continue to work out our salvation in fear and trembling, for it is God who works in you to will and to act in order to fulfill his good purpose." For me, this has been an incredibly difficult concept to grasp. But I have learnt a few things on this journey and can confidently say that God is ok with your questions, your doubts, and your fears. Believe it or not, he is not bothered at all. It is only when you are courageous enough to put these things on the table and meet with God that you realise his heart is, and has always been, for you.

## THE DOOR TO MY HEART

Faith in action is not a onetime response. It is a daily process through which we connect on a deeper, more intimate level with God. It is common for God to allow us to process things in layers. Sometimes we feel as though we have already covered this ground, but we need to trust that our God knows us more deeply than we know ourselves. And this was true for me. Despite surrendering in April 2023, in early 2024, I once again felt the need to express my thoughts and response to the Lord through painting. I sensed Jesus was knocking on the door of my heart and that he wanted to shine a light on those areas I had not yet surrendered, or that required a deeper level of surrender. This painting is called **"The door to my heart"** and reflects the ongoing nature of my journey towards intimacy with Christ and complete surrender.

**8. The door to my heart**

The truth is, this battle for my identity and my salvation has severely wounded me. The fight was incredibly severe, and the damage done was real and long lasting. Killing the CEO required a deep level of separation, of diffusion, if you like. And this often left scarring and nagging pain. The deep-felt pain included the realisation that I was wrong. I had thought I had been living life and serving the Lord with a pure heart and a clean conscience, but the truth was, I had been living a lie. The CEO was a false identity, a lie. Knowing that I had lived completely fused with the CEO hurts.

## PAIN AND DISAPPOINTMENT

I was deeply disappointed in myself. How could I have let this happen? How could I be so foolish? How could I have burned out? I was disappointed with almost everything. My physical body had let me down. How could I not have energy? Why could I not perform like I used to? Professionally I was disappointed with losing my job, my role, and my title; I had worked so hard for these things. Financially, even after all these years and all the work, I was not where I wanted to be. And socially it disappointed me to realise that I was not the person I wanted to be. I suspect it would be close to impossible not to feel a level of disappointment here after going through a journey like this.

However, pain and disappointment are not the end of the story. They are just two more things that I needed to surrender to the Lord. And my journal entry from 5th January 2024 tells the story well.

### 5th January 2024

*'Father, with this painting, I have heard you knocking on the door of my inmost parts. **This door represents pain and disappointment.** I am opening the door, and I invite you to shine your light into this room. Please clean my house and wash my heart clean. Let your light shine in me and through me. Please don't leave stuff there, Lord. I know that my "self" fights hard. I give you permission to shine your light on the pain and the disappointment, so you can usher it out of my life and clean this room completely. Wash me with your blood and let your healing ointment soothe my soul. **Thank you, Lord, I know I can trust you to be gentle and kind.'***

## GRATITUDE, GRACE AND FREEDOM

I can confidently and humbly say that I am now grateful for everything that has happened in my life. Yes, even this last part of the journey. Perhaps, especially for this last part of the journey. When my friends, colleagues and mentors first suggested that one day, I would be grateful for this journey, I honestly thought they had rocks in their head. But as I sit here today writing, I am truly grateful. And I am free. By acting on my faith and surrendering my life to Christ, I have lost nothing of real value and yet I have gained everything that is priceless. I used to be lost, but now I am found.

Life is large again. And by the grace of God, I am free to be Darren.

---

### REFLECTION

**Leadership Lessons**

- Faith is agreement with God
- Faith in action is to thank him for allowing you to breathe and to follow his plan for your life
- Trust God to answer your prayers the way he deems fit
  - It is highly probable that this will not be exactly the way you want the prayer answered
- God will use your skills and abilities for his glory
- Our greatest freedoms can come from the tightest parameters
- When you hear God knocking at the door of your heart – open it

Please be aware, this work is not a one-time action. Surrendering and living your life in agreement with God is a daily choice. This is how we work out our salvation daily. Who is in control of your life today?

---

Where is God revealing a deeper, more expansive truth to you through his word?

How are you experiencing life to the full? Spend some time with the Lord and ask him to open your eyes, ears and heart to his message and the reason for your current season.

Is God knocking on the door of your heart? Are there any rooms that are still locked? Will you open the door and let the light shine in?

Are there any areas where you are still feeling pain?

Are there any areas where you have been or are now disappointed?

Will you allow God to shine a light in your heart and heal these areas?

## *Journal Entries January – September 2024*

### *21st February, 2024*

*It has been some time since my last reflection. However, this has not meant a lack of reflection. Over the last couple of months, I have spent considerable time editing my book. This has enabled me to process and re-process different parts of my journey. The truth remains however, that un-reflected times can be danger-ous times. In the last few weeks, I have felt really good. On numerous occasions I have commented to others that it feels like my energy is returning. However, the problem is the speed at which I revert to what I can do and what I can control. The internal belief, that I have got things under control. I am reminded that the Beast loves to work and will always be a part of my story.*

*I have also heard some of my conversation, and despite having full confidence that God will supply all our needs and provide financially for us, I have become more conscious of needing to procure work that contributes income. We have a never-ending series of bills, which is just normal, but my focus quickly turns to what I can do. It is such a subtle shift that in the past would have gone unchecked. I know God has got it under control. My faith is in him. It is not wrong for me to bring my requests and needs before him. But the lack of rest comes when I try to meet the needs or fill the gap myself so to speak.*

*Oh, and one last genuine reminder that things are not fully back. I needed a new script from the doctor for my antidepressant medication. I had intended to speak with him about beginning the process of reducing the dose. But by the time I was on the phone with him, I realised that this would not be a wise decision just yet. Perhaps, God's way of keeping the thorn in my side and ensuring I continue to rely on him, and not my own strength.*

### 4th March, 2024

*There are things on my mind, and I know I am pushing to get them done. While I am saying the right things, I think my motives have slipped into the wrong gear. Until this point, I have been resting in God and fully trusting in his provision. But as time goes on and I have been feeling better, it is almost as if I am saying to God that I'm good now, just let me loose and let the work come in. The Beast is waking up again. I am so quick to think that I am ok, and I can do it.*

*I know God will provide. I have complete rest and confidence in this, but I have been trying to force things along and consequently, I am struggling.*

*'Father God, I turn to you today. You are the King of Kings, the Almighty. Forgive me once again for my rebellious ways and my selfish habits. Lord, I surrender and submit to you again. I choose to rest in you today. Lead me and guide me, Lord. Help me to live your way.'*

**14th March, 2024**

***Well, well, well... My last day of being 49!***

*It is one of those strange kind of days - 50 is a milestone in anyone's book and it is one that sometimes comes with a realistic acknowledgment of truth... I am getting older.*

*But I am not old. 50 is the new 40, right? To be honest, I am not that bothered about it. It just is and I am quite proud of it.*

*Thinking back over the last few weeks and the challenge is still real. Every day, I have had to consciously decide how to handle things. It is important for me to not only be aware of what is going on but also to make good decisions consistently.*

*God has been good and is answering my prayers. He has provided three leads for some potential work, which is just fantastic. Thank you, Lord, for knowing me and what I can handle. I pray that all these pieces of work will come to fruition and enable us to move forward.*

**22nd May, 2024**

*Spent some time with the Lord this morning – a little overdue. I have noticed that I have been pushing myself a little. I am keen to get forward traction with my book and the associated training material but am sort of going on my own thoughts and agenda. There are financial questions to be answered, and I am a little tired this morning. Nothing new here. I have been feeling quite good overall and appear to be bouncing reasonably well, which is great. However, if I have learned one thing, it is not to get too far ahead of myself. So, after reading for a while, I stopped and ask the Lord what he wanted to talk about.*

### 29th July, 2024

*I noticed my fatigue was really high over the weekend, and also the previous weekend. Mentally, this remains a concern as it reminds me that the burnout/ the low, is never far away. Just when I think I am going ok, I get a reality check. Every time I have thought about coming off my medication, I have had a scenario that has caused additional fatigue, and I am reminded that I am not yet 100%. On the good side of things, I am aware of my body within hours, not days or weeks, as used to be the case. In most situations, I can adjust actions and thinking within hours, or at least address my thinking and identify the cause within a day or two. Also, fatigue instantly affects my decision making and is like an early warning system for something not being quite right.*

### 13th August, 2024

*Getting back in the habit of journalling. It never ceases to amaze me how quickly I resort to thinking I am all good and don't need to process my thoughts. Anyway, here I am… sitting at the Coffee Club while my car is getting checked for an oil leak.*

*It is now August, and the year is flying by at a rate of knots. There has been quite a bit going on, including limited work and a significantly slowed flow of finances. But I know God will provide. The family is going mostly well although there have been some relationship changes.*

*'Lord Jesus, you can see all that is happening and all that is on my mind. Thank you for the opportunity to stop, think and connect with you. I give all these concerns over to you. I lay them at the foot of the cross, and I release my control of them to you. I surrender. Your will be done in every situation, even the ones I have forgotten to mention. I ask you to lead and guide me so that I can live and act in accordance with your will. And as I do that, I know you will bless the work of my hands. Thank you for your words of encouragement from Isaiah about doing a new thing. I trust you, Lord, and I commit my path to you, my family to you and my finances to you. Fill me with your spirit and lead me today.'*

### 3rd September, 2024

*Things are ramping up in terms of busyness at the moment. I feel my stress and anxiety increasing, and this feeling worsens when I see the dark bags under my eyes in the mirror. I have not been able to shake the fatigue in the last few weeks. This morning, I succeeded in spending some time with the Lord, even though there was significant internal noise and the need to continually remind God of my position—as if he is unaware.*

*Bottom line, I think the message I need to learn (over and over) is that it is not about me. It is not about what I can produce or do. It is always about God and what he can do. I know I can trust him, and I know he will come through. I am just a little anxious, given the current circumstances.*

*'So today, I come to you Lord and sincerely repent of my self-righteousness and pride that says I can do it, it is up to me. You have proven repeatedly that if*

*not for you, I can do nothing. You are my provider. Please forgive me, Lord. Father God, you know all that I need and all that my family needs. I lay these needs and my struggles and sin at the foot of the cross and choose to worship you. Thank you for your kindness. Thank you for allowing me to live today and for listening to me. Please provide all that we need and shine your light on the way forward.'*

*Thank you, Lord.*

# EPILOGUE

Thank you for taking the time to engage with my story. It has been long and difficult, messy, and complicated, but in all honesty, I wouldn't change a thing. For the first time in my life, I am seeing things clearly. I am aware of what is going on in my body, and how I react in certain situations. Thanks to the help of the Lord, my wife, my family, my colleagues, and yes even Virgil, I have developed a new set of core beliefs, values, attitudes, skills, and behaviours. In fact, I have found out who I am. I have found Darren. My identity is no longer tied to the role of CEO, but is now anchored in the love of God, the Creator of the universe. My purpose is to do his will. To reflect and reveal Christ in the way I live so that others may come and follow him and have a relationship with him.

I am extremely grateful that God has walked with me on this transformative journey, and that he continues to walk with me into the future. The journey is by no means over. There will be further mountains to climb, challenges to overcome, mindsets to change and beliefs to renew. However, I am now looking forward to a future with excitement, anticipation, and abundance rather than one of stress, depression, and anxiety. And it is my hope that as you have connected with my story, you too might be encouraged to seek God and find your true identity and purpose.

**Now finally, before you put this down, please consider:**

1.  Have you been living as the CEO of your own life?
2.  Is your identity tied to a role, or position or financial status?
3.  Are your core beliefs accurate, true, and sufficient to live a life of maturity and significance?
4.  Have you experienced any of the physical or mental symptoms described in this book?
    a.  If so, what have you done about these? Please don't be afraid to seek help. You need it, and it is good.
5.  Who is in your circle? Do you have people you can trust and call on? Do you have people who can walk alongside you, support you, and hold you accountable?
    a.  Have you considered a mentor, or life coach, counselor, therapist, or pastor?
6.  How do you process the events of your life? Do you have positive habits such as journalling, exercising, painting, writing, and connecting socially with trusted people?
7.  Are there any habits that you need to adjust or stop completely? Are you struggling with addiction of any kind?
8.  Do you know God? What steps can you take to find him for yourself?

My wife and I have established our company, **LifeRoad Enterprises Pty Ltd**, with the primary purpose of helping to move people forward. We have developed a range of products and services that enable us to walk alongside individuals, teams, and organisations on their journey of transformation. These include - executive coaching, reflective expeditions and retreats, public speaking engagements, team building and leadership training, consulting, and strategic planning.

The challenges and issues discussed in *Killing the CEO* are often a central feature in our programs, and our tailored delivery ensures that we address specific needs. Our experiential programs enhance engagement and learning, and our practical tools and resources help facilitate ongoing application of the lessons learnt. If you would like more information about these products and services, please visit our website **liferoad.com.au**

# ACKNOWLEDGEMENTS

First and foremost, I would like to thank my Lord and Saviour Jesus Christ. Finding you again in and through this journey has been the whole point. I am so grateful for your wisdom, your kindness, and your gentle way of leading me through. Thank you for never leaving me or forsaking me. Thank you for being true to your word and for being someone I can truly trust.

To my best friend and my wife, Yvette – thank you, and I love you. I want to acknowledge your amazing solidarity and wisdom. You have been my rock, and I am just so grateful for your capacity to walk with me. Yvette, thank you for giving me the time and space I required. Thank you for your grace and incredible ability to help me articulate my emotions. Thank you for reading and editing this book and my journal entries, and for both crying and laughing with me and at me in the process. And finally, thank you for allowing me the time to go on the journey. I love you, babe!

I would also like to thank my sons, Sam, Jack and Harry and my daughter Bella. I love you all so much. You have all walked this journey with me and seen the highs and the lows. I am just so grateful to have mature young people who know how to show genuine love and care. I am also grateful for your collectively cheeky sense of humour as you remind me to smile when

I take my happy pill, or when you may have outlasted me on the basketball court.

Thank you, Virgil. Sitting on your couch was, at first, one of the most terrifying experiences of my life. Your exceptional listening skills, powers of observation and genuine desire to help me have completely changed my life and my perception of the art of psychology. Thank you for your patience. I know it was longer than either of us expected, and truth be told, I might still visit you in the future. Thank you for respecting my faith and encouraging me on the way forward.

I would also like to acknowledge and thank the Board of Directors and Executive at the outdoor education company where I was CEO. You made every effort to walk alongside me, support me, and see me restored. You also acted with integrity, authenticity, and generosity in all the decisions you made. Your friendship, wisdom and support mean the world to me. Additionally, I would like to thank the staff in general. You were always supportive and encouraging, even when the path ahead and my role in it were unclear.

To my parents Ken and Jenny and in-laws Jo and Wayne, my brothers and sisters and extended family, thank you so much for your genuine love, care, and prayers. You gave me the space I needed and allowed me to process things in my time and supported me along the way.

Whilst on this journey, I kept my inner circle small and tight, but I would particularly like to acknowledge Jeremy and Phoebe for their friendship, wisdom, and support. Yvette and I are so grateful to have you in our lives. Jeremy, you made it safe for me to accept taking medication and helped me to see a better way. Phoebe, your genuine interest and support for me have been such a blessing, but most of all your love and support for Yvette has helped more than you will ever know. Thank you both.

To all those involved in the production of this book, the associated training material, creating our website and social media presence and digital capacity, thank you. Your insight, wisdom, capacity, and direction have helped significantly. Thank you also for your patience with the many adjustments and amendments.

Finally, to you, the reader, thank you for purchasing this book and taking the time to connect with my story. I sincerely hope it resonated with you and that in some way it might help you live life in the fullness of God's truth as you find your true identity, purpose, calling and fulfillment in relationship with Christ.

God Bless,
Darren

# REFERENCES

Anderson R, J. &. (2016). *Mastering Leadership.* New Jersey: John Wiley & Sons.

Barker k, B. D. (1995). *The NIV Study Bible* (10th Anniversary Edition ed.). Grand Rapids: Zondervan Publishing House.

Bono. (2022). *Surrender.* London: Penguin Random House UK.

Bryant-Smith, R. &. (2018). *Fix Your Team.* Brisbane: John Wiley & Sons Australia Pty Ltd.

Collins, J. (2001). *Good To Great.* Sydney: Random House Australia Pty Ltd.

Karpman Stephen, B. (1968). *Wikipedia.* Retrieved September 25, 2023, from https://en.wikipedia.org/wiki/Karpman_drama_triangle

Nieuwhof, C. (2018). *Didn't See it Coming.* New York: WaterBrook - Penguin Random House LLC.

# IMAGES AND TABLES

www.ingramcontent.com/pod-product-compliance
Lightning Source LLC
Chambersburg PA
CBHW030924090426
42737CB00007B/310